Azure Architect's Playbook: Design for Scale: 1st Edition

First Edition

Preface

In an era defined by rapid digital transformation, the need for scalable, reliable, and secure cloud architecture has never been more critical. This book, *Azure Architect's Playbook: Design for Scale: 1st Edition*, is crafted for aspiring and seasoned architects looking to harness Microsoft Azure's vast capabilities to design solutions that not only meet today's demands but are also future-ready.

From foundational concepts to advanced architectural patterns, this book takes a practical approach to Azure cloud design. We begin with the principles of scalable cloud architecture and examine the role of the Azure architect in enabling enterprise growth. We then explore core Azure services, the underlying design considerations, and how to structure identities, regions, and resource management for scale.

As the chapters progress, readers will be guided through designing compute, storage, and database solutions that can dynamically adapt to workload demands. We'll dive into networking strategies that ensure high availability and connectivity across regions and hybrid environments. Security, identity, and governance are treated as first-class citizens, with detailed strategies for compliance and secure scale.

The book also emphasizes the importance of operational excellence through monitoring, cost management, and DevOps automation. It culminates with advanced hyperscale patterns, real-world case studies from multiple industries, and a forward-looking view of Azure's roadmap, including AI, edge computing, and sustainability.

Whether you're leading digital transformation in an enterprise, building your first hyperscale system, or simply want to deepen your knowledge of Azure, this book serves as both a comprehensive guide and a practical reference for creating resilient, performant, and future-proof architectures.

Table of Contents

Chapter 1: Introduction to Scalable Cloud Architecture

The Evolution of Cloud Architecture

Cloud computing has fundamentally transformed how organizations build, deploy, and scale digital services. Initially driven by the promise of cost savings and operational efficiency, the cloud has evolved into a cornerstone of innovation and digital agility. To appreciate the modern capabilities of Microsoft Azure, it's essential to understand how cloud architecture itself has evolved over time.

From On-Premises to Virtualization

Before cloud platforms like Azure existed, enterprises relied heavily on physical infrastructure. Data centers were equipped with dedicated servers, network hardware, and storage appliances. Scaling required the procurement of additional hardware, often resulting in over-provisioning or resource starvation. Capacity planning was based on peak traffic estimates, leading to inefficiencies and sunk costs.

The advent of virtualization in the early 2000s changed this paradigm. Technologies like VMware allowed multiple virtual machines (VMs) to run on a single physical server, improving hardware utilization and resource flexibility. However, managing virtualized infrastructure still demanded significant manual oversight, lacked elasticity, and required substantial capital investment.

Rise of Public Cloud Platforms

Public cloud providers like Microsoft, Amazon, and Google introduced a new model: Infrastructure as a Service (IaaS). Azure enabled organizations to provision compute, storage, and network resources on-demand with pay-as-you-go pricing. This shift unlocked unprecedented scalability and speed, making it possible to deploy global services without owning a single server.

With Azure, developers and architects no longer needed to manage hardware or anticipate resource needs months in advance. Instead, workloads could scale dynamically based on demand, and high availability became a feature of the platform itself.

From IaaS to PaaS and Serverless

While IaaS abstracted hardware, Platform as a Service (PaaS) went a step further by abstracting operating systems and runtime environments. Services like Azure App Service allowed teams to deploy applications without managing the underlying VM or patching OS-level vulnerabilities.

The evolution continued with serverless computing. Azure Functions and Logic Apps removed the need to provision or scale infrastructure entirely. Developers could now write event-driven code that scales instantly, based on triggers like HTTP requests, timers, or message queues.

This evolution enabled architectural shifts from monolithic systems to distributed, decoupled, and event-driven designs. Cloud-native patterns emerged, emphasizing scalability, fault tolerance, and microservice decomposition.

Impact on Enterprise Architecture

Enterprises began to reorganize their architecture principles around the capabilities of the cloud. Traditional three-tier applications evolved into globally distributed systems with autoscaling APIs, multi-region failover, and containerized workloads orchestrated by Azure Kubernetes Service (AKS).

This architectural evolution required a new role: the cloud architect. This professional blends deep technical expertise with business alignment, ensuring that cloud solutions meet performance, compliance, and scalability needs. In Azure, the architect's toolbox includes over 200 services, from networking and identity to databases and AI.

Evolution of Azure-Specific Services

Microsoft Azure has mirrored—and often led—the evolution of cloud services. Here's a brief timeline of major architectural innovations on the platform:

- **2010–2013**: Azure launched with core services like Web Roles, SQL Azure, and Blob Storage. IaaS VMs were introduced, making Azure a true hybrid platform.

- **2014–2016**: Azure Resource Manager (ARM) modernized resource provisioning. Azure AD became central to identity and access.

- **2017–2019**: AKS, Azure Functions, and Cosmos DB matured, enabling microservices and serverless architectures at scale.

- **2020–2023**: Azure Arc, Azure Synapse, and Durable Functions brought hybrid, analytical, and stateful serverless capabilities.

- **2024 and beyond**: Azure's AI, machine learning, and edge computing services are transforming how scalable architectures are conceived and delivered.

Common Challenges and Solutions

Scalability doesn't come without challenges. Architects must consider:

- **State Management**: Stateless services scale well; stateful ones require careful design (e.g., Redis, Cosmos DB).

- **Service Boundaries**: Microservices must be isolated yet integrated via APIs or queues.

- **Concurrency and Throttling**: Azure services have quotas; knowing how to design for throughput is essential.

- **Cold Starts**: Serverless functions can suffer latency. Solutions include pre-warming or premium tiers.

- **Cost Escalation**: Autoscaling can increase cost rapidly without observability and budget alerts.

Design Patterns Driving Evolution

Azure architects today apply design patterns that emerged from this evolution:

- **CQRS (Command Query Responsibility Segregation)** for split-read/write scaling

- **Event Sourcing** for reliable distributed transactions

- **Bulkhead and Circuit Breaker** for service isolation

- **Cache-Aside** for improved performance

- **Strangler Fig** for gradual modernization of legacy systems

These patterns, often combined with tools like Azure API Management, Event Grid, Service Bus, and Key Vault, make it possible to build resilient systems that scale predictably.

Future Trajectory of Cloud Architecture

Looking forward, several trends are likely to shape the next stage of architectural evolution:

- **AI-Integrated Workloads**: Models are being embedded directly into APIs and applications. Azure OpenAI Services and Azure ML will be architectural building blocks.

- **Edge-to-Cloud**: With Azure Stack and Azure IoT, compute is moving closer to data sources. Architectures must now consider edge orchestration and synchronization.

- **Zero Trust Security**: Identity-first design is shifting how access control is implemented, particularly in multi-cloud and hybrid environments.

- **Green Architecture**: Azure's sustainability goals influence architecture choices like serverless and ephemeral compute to reduce energy use.

In short, the evolution of cloud architecture is far from complete. Each year introduces new services, capabilities, and challenges. As Azure continues to mature, architects must continuously adapt—balancing scalability, cost, performance, and compliance.

The following chapters build on this foundation, guiding you through each architectural domain within Azure, helping you create systems that are not only scalable, but truly cloud-native and enterprise-ready.

Key Principles of Scalability

Scalability is the capacity of a system to handle growth—in users, data, transactions, or processes—without compromising performance, reliability, or cost-efficiency. In cloud architecture, scalability is not a singular design feature; it is a set of principles that, when applied thoughtfully, enable your application or platform to dynamically adapt to changing demands. In Azure, achieving true scalability requires an understanding of these core principles, backed by a deep knowledge of the platform's tools and limitations.

Horizontal vs. Vertical Scaling

One of the foundational principles is understanding the two major types of scaling:

- **Vertical Scaling (Scaling Up)**: Increases the capacity of a single resource—e.g., upgrading a VM from 4 vCPUs to 16 vCPUs. It's simple but limited by hardware caps and introduces a single point of failure.

- **Horizontal Scaling (Scaling Out)**: Adds more instances of a resource—e.g., running multiple app servers behind a load balancer. This method is typically more scalable and fault-tolerant.

In Azure, most modern applications should favor horizontal scaling wherever possible. Azure App Services, Azure Kubernetes Service (AKS), and Virtual Machine Scale Sets (VMSS) all support horizontal scaling with native integration into load balancing and health-check mechanisms.

Example of setting auto-scaling in an Azure App Service using ARM template:

```json
{
  "type": "Microsoft.Insights/autoscalesettings",
  "name": "autoscale-rule",
  "properties": {
    "targetResourceUri":          "[resourceId('Microsoft.Web/sites',
parameters('appName'))]",
    "enabled": true,
    "autoscaleSettingResourceName": "autoscale-rule",
    "profiles": [
```

```
{
    "name": "AutoScaleProfile",
    "capacity": {
        "minimum": "1",
        "maximum": "10",
        "default": "2"
    },
    "rules": [
        {
            "metricTrigger": {
                "metricName": "CpuPercentage",
                "metricNamespace": "",
                "metricResourceUri":
"[resourceId('Microsoft.Web/sites', parameters('appName'))]",
                "timeGrain": "PT1M",
                "statistic": "Average",
                "timeWindow": "PT5M",
                "timeAggregation": "Average",
                "operator": "GreaterThan",
                "threshold": 70
            },
            "scaleAction": {
                "direction": "Increase",
                "type": "ChangeCount",
                "value": "1",
                "cooldown": "PT1M"
            }
        }
    ]
}
}
```

This configuration allows the application to scale out when CPU usage exceeds 70% for a continuous 5-minute window, with a cooldown of 1 minute.

Stateless Design

Statelessness is one of the most important principles in building scalable systems. A stateless service does not retain any session data between requests. This allows for seamless scaling because any instance can serve any request. In contrast, stateful services require session affinity, which reduces elasticity and introduces complexity.

In Azure, designing stateless applications means using distributed caches (e.g., Azure Cache for Redis) or persistent data stores (e.g., Azure SQL Database, Cosmos DB) to manage session or application state.

Best practices for stateless design include:

- Avoid using local file systems for user or app data.

- Store session data in Redis or Cosmos DB.

- Use tokens (e.g., JWT) for authentication instead of in-memory sessions.

Example pseudocode of token-based stateless auth:

```
// Express.js middleware (Node.js) for stateless JWT validation
const jwt = require('jsonwebtoken');
function authenticateToken(req, res, next) {
  const token = req.headers['authorization'];
  if (!token) return res.sendStatus(401);
  jwt.verify(token, process.env.ACCESS_TOKEN_SECRET, (err, user) => {
    if (err) return res.sendStatus(403);
    req.user = user;
    next();
  });
}
```

This enables any instance to authenticate any user, making the service scalable and resilient to instance loss.

Load Distribution and Balancing

A system is not scalable if it lacks effective load distribution. Azure provides several load balancing options, including:

- **Azure Load Balancer**: Layer 4 (TCP/UDP) load distribution, best for VM traffic.

- **Azure Application Gateway**: Layer 7 (HTTP/HTTPS) with path-based routing and SSL offloading.

- **Azure Front Door**: Global load balancing with health probes and geo-distribution.

Choosing the right load balancer is critical. For microservices, you may combine them—for example, using Front Door for global routing and Application Gateway for internal routing and WAF.

Design considerations for load balancing:

- Use health probes to detect and remove failing instances.

- Deploy multiple instances across Availability Zones.

- Use sticky sessions only when unavoidable and with caution.

Resource Pooling and Multi-Tenancy

For scalable SaaS architectures, **multi-tenancy** allows a single application instance to serve multiple customers (tenants), efficiently sharing compute and storage. Azure provides mechanisms like:

- Tenant-level data isolation with separate databases or containers.

- Shared hosting with row-level security in SQL.

- Custom domains and Azure AD B2C for authentication per tenant.

Effective multi-tenant design must balance performance, isolation, and cost. For example, in Cosmos DB, each tenant can be mapped to a different partition key for performance isolation.

```
{
  "partitionKey": {
    "paths": ["/tenantId"],
    "kind": "Hash"
  }
}
```

This approach ensures write and read scalability per tenant.

Elasticity

Elasticity is the system's ability to shrink and grow with demand automatically. Unlike scalability, which describes capacity, elasticity is about responsiveness and efficiency. Azure services like App Service Plans, Azure Functions, and VMSS offer auto-scaling configurations based on:

- CPU, memory, queue length

- Schedule (e.g., night vs. peak hours)

- Custom metrics (via Azure Monitor)

Elasticity improves cost-efficiency and user experience. When paired with observability and automation, it allows you to meet SLAs without overprovisioning.

Asynchronous Processing and Queuing

Scalable architectures favor asynchronous processing for tasks that are long-running, non-critical, or resource-intensive. Azure provides a variety of tools for this:

- **Azure Service Bus**: Reliable message broker for high-throughput needs.

- **Azure Queue Storage**: Simple, cost-effective queuing.

- **Azure Event Grid**: Event-based communication.

- **Azure Event Hubs**: Real-time data ingestion for streaming scenarios.

Use cases include:

- Order processing

- Image or video encoding

- Sending notifications

- Updating analytics dashboards

Pattern example:

1. Web app receives order and pushes it to Service Bus.

2. Worker Service listens to queue and processes payment.

3. Azure Function picks up successful payment and sends email.

Benefits include decoupling, improved response times, and parallel processing, all of which are pillars of scalable design.

Observability and Feedback Loops

Scalability must be monitored and adjusted continuously. Observability ensures that your architecture adapts to real-world usage patterns. Azure Monitor, Log Analytics, and Application Insights offer a comprehensive toolset for:

- Custom metrics (e.g., transactions per second)

- Distributed tracing

- Anomaly detection

- Alerting and autoscale triggers

For example, set alerts to notify when CPU usage exceeds 85% or when throughput on Cosmos DB approaches RU limits. Use these signals to adjust scaling policies or tune performance.

Example Kusto Query (KQL) to track CPU:

```
Perf
| where ObjectName == "Processor" and CounterName == "% Processor
Time"
| summarize avg(CounterValue) by bin(TimeGenerated, 5m), Computer
```

This allows real-time dashboards to identify performance bottlenecks.

Idempotency and Retry Logic

In highly scalable systems, retrying operations is common due to network delays or temporary failures. However, this can lead to duplicate operations if not handled correctly.

Ensure **idempotency**—that is, multiple identical operations produce the same result. For example, submitting a payment twice should not result in duplicate charges.

Strategies:

- Use unique operation IDs to detect duplicates.

- Store operation state and timestamps.

- Apply locking or deduplication logic in your database or queue.

Throttling and Backpressure

Every service has limits. Scalable designs must anticipate and handle throttling gracefully. Azure services like Cosmos DB, Event Hubs, and Azure Functions will return 429 (Too Many Requests) responses when limits are exceeded.

Best practices:

- Use retry-after headers to delay retries.

- Implement exponential backoff and jitter.

- Monitor quotas and provision capacity accordingly.

Example retry logic with exponential backoff (pseudocode):

```
async function retryWithBackoff(fn, maxRetries) {
  for (let i = 0; i < maxRetries; i++) {
    try {
      return await fn();
    } catch (error) {
      const delay = Math.pow(2, i) * 100 + Math.random() * 100;
      await new Promise(res => setTimeout(res, delay));
    }
  }
  throw new Error('Max retries exceeded');
}
```

Summary

Scalability is not a checkbox; it's a spectrum of principles that must be deeply embedded into the architecture, development, deployment, and monitoring of your systems. In Azure, leveraging platform-native services to implement statelessness, asynchronous patterns, auto-scaling, load balancing, and observability ensures your solution can adapt in real-time to business needs.

Designing for scale starts with understanding your workload and user patterns and applying the right principles early in the architecture. By following the practices outlined in this section, you set a strong foundation for building scalable systems in Azure that are elastic, efficient, and ready for growth.

Role of the Azure Architect in Enterprise Growth

The Azure Architect plays a pivotal role in shaping the technological trajectory of an enterprise, driving innovation, ensuring scalability, and delivering value through cloud-native design. In the context of enterprise growth, the architect isn't just a technical implementer—they are a strategist, advisor, and enabler. Their influence spans infrastructure, application design, security, governance, cost optimization, and compliance, all of which are critical to sustainable digital transformation.

Beyond Infrastructure: Strategic Thinking

Enterprises today don't move to the cloud merely to reduce costs—they do so to gain agility, resilience, and competitive advantage. The Azure Architect's job is to align cloud strategy with business goals. This begins by deeply understanding:

- The business model and growth drivers
- Key customer experience pain points
- Organizational readiness for digital change
- Existing technical debt and monolithic systems

Armed with this context, the architect designs solutions that scale with business ambition. For instance, a company expanding into international markets may require a multi-region architecture with local data residency, low latency, and multi-language support. The Azure Architect translates these business requirements into a scalable, performant solution using services like Azure Front Door, Azure Cosmos DB with geo-replication, and Azure AD B2C for localized authentication.

Platform Architecture: Building the Foundation

At the heart of every cloud-native enterprise platform is a robust, modular, and reusable architecture. Azure Architects design this foundation by creating reference architectures and reusable landing zones. These include:

- **Management Groups and Subscriptions** for workload separation
- **Resource Groups** for logical organization
- **Azure Policy and Blueprints** for governance and compliance
- **Hub-and-Spoke Network Topology** for scalable networking
- **Shared Services Layer** (e.g., monitoring, identity, DNS)

Example: Hub-and-Spoke VNet topology with shared services

- **Hub VNet**: Houses VPN Gateway, Azure Firewall, and monitoring tools
- **Spoke VNets**: Host workloads like AKS clusters or App Services

- **Peering**: Connects spokes to the hub while isolating each other

- **NSGs and ASGs**: Enforce security boundaries at subnet and VM levels

This model enables fast provisioning of new environments for projects, business units, or regions, without compromising governance or security.

Architectural Review and Solution Validation

As enterprises scale, so do the risks associated with architectural complexity. Azure Architects are responsible for leading **architecture review boards** and conducting **solution validation workshops**. These sessions ensure that each team adheres to organizational standards and architectural principles.

Typical responsibilities during reviews:

- Assessing non-functional requirements (NFRs) like scalability, latency, and uptime

- Validating cost estimates using Azure Pricing Calculator and Azure Cost Management

- Reviewing security posture, including identity management, key storage, and logging

- Enforcing tagging standards and resource naming conventions

- Approving or guiding choices like VM SKUs, database tiers, and scaling policies

Architects use tools like **Azure Well-Architected Review** to benchmark and guide teams. These reviews focus on the five pillars: cost optimization, performance efficiency, reliability, operational excellence, and security.

Designing for Change and Growth

Enterprises are dynamic. New product launches, acquisitions, regulatory changes, and customer demands all require the cloud platform to evolve. Azure Architects design with **change tolerance** in mind. This includes:

- **Loose Coupling**: Using message queues (Service Bus, Event Grid) to decouple systems

- **Service Isolation**: Deploying microservices in separate containers or App Services

- **Infrastructure as Code (IaC)**: Defining environments with ARM, Bicep, or Terraform for repeatability

- **Versioning APIs**: Supporting multiple API versions to avoid breaking changes

Example Terraform configuration for modular deployment:

```
module "network" {
  source               = "./modules/network"
  vnet_name            = "enterprise-vnet"
  address_space        = ["10.0.0.0/16"]
  resource_group_name  = var.resource_group
}

module "aks" {
  source               = "./modules/aks"
  cluster_name         = "prod-aks"
  node_count           = 3
  resource_group_name  = var.resource_group
  vnet_subnet_id       = module.network.subnet_id
}
```

By using modules, the architect ensures reusable, composable environments that scale with organizational needs.

Security as a Core Concern

With growth comes increased exposure. Azure Architects are defenders as much as builders. Security decisions have lasting impact and must be embedded in every architectural layer:

- **Identity and Access**: Design RBAC policies using least privilege. Integrate with Azure AD and Conditional Access.

- **Key Management**: Store secrets in Azure Key Vault with RBAC or managed identities.

- **Perimeter Defense**: Use Application Gateway with WAF and Azure Firewall.

- **Zero Trust**: Ensure every user, device, and app is verified and validated.

Security automation also matters. Architects often implement **policy-as-code** using Azure Policy, enabling automated enforcement of rules such as:

```
{
  "properties": {
    "displayName": "Only allow managed disks",
    "policyRule": {
      "if": {
        "not": {
```

```
        "field": "Microsoft.Compute/disks/sku.name",
        "in": ["Standard_LRS", "Premium_LRS"]
      }
    },
    "then": {
      "effect": "deny"
    }
  }
 }
}
```

This policy prevents developers from deploying unapproved disk types, enforcing consistency across environments.

Data-Driven Decision Making

Growth-oriented enterprises rely heavily on data. Azure Architects must support data-driven decisions by:

- Designing scalable data platforms using Azure Synapse, Data Lake, and Databricks

- Architecting pipelines for real-time and batch ingestion using Data Factory and Event Hubs

- Ensuring data classification and lifecycle policies are applied

- Enabling analytics and BI with Power BI integration

Architects also ensure that data solutions scale with business expansion—across regions, workloads, and governance boundaries—while respecting compliance like GDPR or HIPAA.

Cost Optimization and Financial Stewardship

A scalable architecture is incomplete without **cost efficiency**. Azure Architects work closely with FinOps and procurement teams to:

- Analyze usage patterns and recommend Reserved Instances or Savings Plans

- Set up Azure Budgets and Alerts

- Implement cost showback/chargeback models for departments

- Optimize underutilized resources, such as idle VMs, oversized SKUs, or stale disks

- Use spot VMs and serverless where applicable

Architects often review Azure Advisor recommendations and provide remediation plans to project teams.

Coaching and Cultural Transformation

Enterprise growth in the cloud is not just technical—it's cultural. Azure Architects play a critical role in coaching teams to adopt DevOps, Agile, and continuous innovation. They promote:

- Adoption of Azure DevOps or GitHub Actions for CI/CD pipelines
- Shift-left security using static code analysis and policy scans
- Cloud Center of Excellence (CCoE) frameworks
- InnerSource and code reuse across departments
- Upskilling through hands-on labs, sandbox environments, and certification paths

An effective architect doesn't gatekeep—they **empower**.

Managing Complexity with Blueprints and Landing Zones

Architects use **landing zones** to accelerate secure cloud adoption while maintaining guardrails. Azure Landing Zones are pre-configured environments that incorporate best practices for networking, identity, security, and operations.

Key elements of a landing zone:

- Policy enforcement (e.g., no public IPs on VMs)
- Logging and monitoring baseline
- Network architecture with firewalls and DNS
- Identity integration with hybrid AD or Azure AD

Azure Blueprints let architects define reusable templates with RBAC assignments, policy definitions, and resource templates.

```
{
  "properties": {
    "displayName": "Enterprise Baseline",
```

```
    "description":     "Applies     core     security     and     networking
configurations.",
    "targetScope": "subscription",
    "parameters": { },
    "resourceGroups": {
      "monitoring-rg": {
        "name": "monitoring-rg",
        "location": "eastus"
      }
    },
    "policies": [
      {
        "policyDefinitionId":
"/providers/Microsoft.Authorization/policyDefinitions/deny-public-
ip",
        "parameters": {}
      }
    ]
  }
}
```

This makes onboarding new teams or workloads consistent, fast, and compliant.

Leading Through Innovation

Finally, the Azure Architect is a **technology leader**. They stay abreast of Azure's evolving roadmap—AI integrations, confidential computing, Project Bicep enhancements, Arc-enabled services—and identify which innovations align with business value.

For example:

- Using Azure OpenAI Service to power intelligent chatbots for customer support

- Leveraging Azure Arc to manage multi-cloud Kubernetes workloads

- Deploying edge solutions with Azure Stack HCI for manufacturing

These decisions accelerate transformation and ensure the enterprise remains competitive.

Conclusion

The Azure Architect is more than a cloud engineer. They are the stewards of enterprise agility, security, and innovation. As businesses scale, they depend on the architect's vision and execution to maintain resilience, contain costs, and deliver exceptional digital experiences.

By balancing technical rigor with strategic foresight, Azure Architects enable sustainable enterprise growth—creating platforms that adapt, scale, and evolve in harmony with business objectives. Their role is dynamic, influential, and indispensable in today's cloud-first world.

Chapter 2: Foundations of Microsoft Azure for Architects

Core Azure Services and Their Architecture Relevance

Understanding Microsoft Azure's core services is essential for architects designing scalable, resilient, and cost-effective solutions. Azure offers a rich ecosystem of over 200 services, but successful architecture doesn't depend on mastering them all—it depends on knowing which **core services** are foundational, how they interact, and when to use them.

This section explores the building blocks of Azure that every architect must be fluent in: compute, storage, networking, identity, databases, integration, and management. We'll not only define each service type but also analyze architectural implications and best practices for using them in enterprise-grade solutions.

Compute Services

Azure provides a diverse set of compute services to handle varied workload requirements. These services enable different levels of abstraction and control.

Azure Virtual Machines (VMs)

VMs are Infrastructure-as-a-Service (IaaS) offerings allowing full control over the operating system and runtime. Architects typically use VMs for:

- Legacy workloads

- Custom configurations (e.g., specific OS or security agents)

- Lift-and-shift migrations

- Applications requiring kernel-level access

Architectural considerations:

- Select VM series based on workload (e.g., D-series for general-purpose, E-series for memory-intensive workloads).

- Use **Availability Sets** or **Availability Zones** for HA.

- Attach **Managed Disks** and leverage **Azure Backup** for resilience.

- Employ **VM Scale Sets (VMSS)** for horizontal scaling.

Example Bicep snippet for provisioning a VM:

```
resource vm 'Microsoft.Compute/virtualMachines@2023-03-01' = {
  name: 'webserver-vm'
  location: resourceGroup().location
  properties: {
    hardwareProfile: {
      vmSize: 'Standard_D2s_v3'
    }
    storageProfile: {
      osDisk: {
        createOption: 'FromImage'
      }
    }
    osProfile: {
      computerName: 'webvm'
      adminUsername: 'azureuser'
    }
    networkProfile: {
      networkInterfaces: [
        {
          id: nic.id
        }
      ]
    }
  }
}
```

Azure App Service

A PaaS offering that simplifies deployment and scaling of web applications. Architects use App Service for:

- REST   APIs

- Websites   and   web   apps

- Mobile   app   backends

Architectural benefits:

- Built-in   autoscaling,   staging   slots,   and   CI/CD   integration.

- Integration with VNETs via Private Endpoint or Hybrid Connections.

- Authentication support via Azure AD, Facebook, Google, etc.

Ideal for projects where the operational overhead of managing infrastructure needs to be minimized.

Azure Kubernetes Service (AKS)

A container orchestration platform offering fine-grained control over deployment, scaling, and service mesh. Architects choose AKS for:

- Microservices and service meshes

- Multi-container application architectures

- Advanced CI/CD and observability scenarios

AKS enables enterprise-grade Kubernetes features such as:

- Node pools with different VM sizes

- Azure CNI integration for custom VNETs

- Use of Helm charts, KEDA for event-based autoscaling

Challenges:

- Steeper learning curve

- Complex upgrades and versioning strategies

Storage Services

Storage is fundamental to every application. Azure provides multiple storage services tailored to different data types and usage patterns.

Azure Blob Storage

Used for unstructured data (images, videos, backups, logs). Architectural use cases:

- Data lakes

- Web content hosting

- Static websites (via $web container)
- Event-driven processing with Event Grid

Key architectural decisions:

- Choose between **Hot**, **Cool**, and **Archive** tiers based on access frequency.
- Use lifecycle rules to automate tiering and deletion.
- Enable versioning and soft delete for resilience.

```
{
  "properties": {
    "deleteRetentionPolicy": {
      "enabled": true,
      "days": 30
    },
    "isVersioningEnabled": true
  }
}
```

Azure Files

Provides SMB/NFS-compatible shared storage. Common use cases:

- Lift-and-shift apps needing file shares
- Multi-node compute jobs accessing the same dataset
- User profile storage in VDI scenarios

Azure Disk Storage

Best for IOPS-intensive workloads like databases and virtual desktop infrastructure.

- Use Ultra Disks for low-latency and high-throughput.
- Combine with VM Scale Sets or Availability Sets for fault tolerance.

Networking Services

Networking connects compute and storage across secure, scalable, and performant topologies.

Azure Virtual Network (VNet)

The foundational construct for networking. Architects configure VNets with subnets, NSGs, route tables, and service endpoints.

Key design principles:

- Isolate by environment (e.g., dev, test, prod)

- Reserve IP ranges using CIDR notation (avoid overlaps for peering)

- Use **Private Endpoints** for PaaS service access without public exposure

Azure Load Balancer vs. Application Gateway

- Use **Azure Load Balancer** for L4 (TCP/UDP) scenarios like database clusters or gaming   servers.

- Use **Application Gateway** for L7 (HTTP/HTTPS) routing, with features like Web Application Firewall (WAF), path-based routing, and SSL offloading.

Azure Front Door

Global, scalable L7 load balancer and content delivery solution. Ideal for:

- Multi-region   app   deployments

- Geographically   distributed   user   bases

- Fast   failover   and   SSL   acceleration

Architects often layer these services: Front Door → Application Gateway → App Service or AKS.

Identity and Access Services

Architecting identity correctly is vital for security and scalability.

Azure Active Directory (AAD)

The central identity service for Azure. Use AAD for:

- Single Sign-On (SSO) and Multi-Factor Authentication (MFA)
- Federated identity with on-prem AD
- App registration and role assignments

Architects design access controls using:

- **RBAC**: Role-Based Access Control for resources.
- **PIM**: Privileged Identity Management for time-based admin access.
- **Managed Identities**: For secure service-to-service communication.

Azure AD B2C

Designed for customer-facing applications. Supports:

- Custom branding
- Identity providers like Facebook, Google, Microsoft
- Policy-based workflows

Example architectural pattern: A SaaS app uses Azure AD B2C for login, stores session in Redis, and uses role claims for UI logic.

Database Services

Azure offers a wide array of databases, each tailored to specific workloads.

Azure SQL Database

Managed relational database with built-in high availability. Use **Elastic Pools** for multi-tenant apps and **Hyperscale** for large databases.

Architectural features:

- Auto-tuning and query performance insights
- Geo-replication
- Threat detection and auditing

Azure Cosmos DB

Globally distributed, multi-model NoSQL database. Supports partitioning, multi-master writes, and various APIs (SQL, MongoDB, Cassandra, Gremlin).

Key architectural implications:

- Design for partitioning early (e.g., `/tenantId`)

- Configure RU/s (Request Units per second) based on performance profiles

- Use Change Feed for event-driven workflows

Azure Database for PostgreSQL/MySQL

Offers flexibility with open-source engines, with features like:

- Flexible server configuration

- Private Link and VNET integration

- Backup and PITR (Point in Time Restore)

Integration Services

Enterprise systems need robust messaging and orchestration. Azure offers:

- **Service Bus**: Enterprise-grade pub/sub messaging with queues and topics.

- **Event Grid**: Lightweight event distribution service.

- **Logic Apps**: Low-code orchestration engine integrating 400+ connectors.

- **Azure Functions**: Event-driven compute, ideal for serverless patterns.

Architectural example: Use Event Grid to trigger an Azure Function when a new file lands in Blob Storage, which then posts metadata to a Service Bus queue for further processing.

Monitoring and Management

Visibility into system performance and availability is essential.

Azure Monitor

Central monitoring service that collects metrics, logs, and traces. Key integrations:

- **Application Insights**: For application-level telemetry

- **Log Analytics**: For querying and diagnostics (KQL)

- **Alerts and Workbooks**: For custom dashboards and alerting logic

Azure Policy and Blueprints

Governance tools for enforcing standards across environments.

Use cases:

- Prevent creation of resources in non-approved regions

- Enforce tag rules and naming conventions

- Ensure encryption at rest is enabled on all storage accounts

Azure Resource Manager (ARM)

The deployment engine for Azure. Architects use ARM templates, Bicep, or Terraform to define infrastructure as code, ensuring repeatable, auditable environments.

Conclusion

Mastering core Azure services is non-negotiable for effective architecture. Each service category—compute, storage, networking, identity, databases, integration, and monitoring—plays a critical role in delivering scalable, secure, and high-performing solutions.

Rather than memorizing every service, successful Azure Architects understand service **capabilities, constraints, and combinations**. They know how to make trade-offs and choose the right services based on business requirements, security posture, and operational needs.

The rest of this book builds on this foundational knowledge, exploring how to apply these services in real-world architectural scenarios to enable enterprise-grade scalability.

Azure Regions, Availability Zones, and SLA Considerations

One of the most strategic decisions an architect makes when designing a cloud solution is determining **where** to deploy it. In Azure, this decision is not just about geography; it impacts **performance**, **resilience**, **compliance**, **latency**, and **cost**. Understanding how Azure's regional infrastructure is structured—and how to leverage Availability Zones and SLAs (Service Level Agreements)—is essential for creating scalable, fault-tolerant, and globally available systems.

Azure Geography Hierarchy

Azure's global infrastructure is divided into several layers of abstraction:

- **Geographies**: Large geopolitical areas (e.g., United States, Europe) often aligned with data sovereignty requirements.

- **Regions**: Specific deployment locations within a geography (e.g., West Europe, East US).

- **Availability Zones**: Physically separated data centers within a region, each with independent power, cooling, and networking.

This hierarchy allows you to design solutions that respect **data residency laws**, achieve **high availability**, and reduce **latency** for global users.

For example:

- **Canada** is a geography.

- **Canada Central** and **Canada East** are two separate regions within that geography.

- **Canada Central** may support multiple Availability Zones.

Selecting the Right Azure Region

Azure spans more than 60+ regions worldwide, more than any other public cloud provider. But not all services are available in every region, and regions differ in cost, performance, and redundancy capabilities.

Key Criteria for Region Selection:

1. **Latency to Users**: Use Azure's latency tools or the Azure Speed Test to determine the closest and fastest region for your users.

2. **Service Availability**: Some services like Azure OpenAI or Confidential Computing are only available in a subset of regions. Use the Azure Products by Region site to verify availability.

3. **Data Residency and Compliance**: GDPR, HIPAA, and other frameworks often dictate where data can be stored or processed. Choose a region aligned with legal requirements.

4. **Redundancy Options**: If your application requires high availability, prioritize regions with **Availability Zones** or pair it with another region for **geo-redundancy**.

5. **Pricing**: Prices for services (VMs, storage, bandwidth) can vary across regions. Refer to the Azure Pricing Calculator to compare costs.

Availability Zones: Designing for Fault Tolerance

Availability Zones (AZs) are the cornerstone of high-availability architecture in Azure. Each zone is an isolated data center within a region. AZs are designed so that a failure in one zone does not affect the others.

Key characteristics:

- Minimum of three zones per AZ-enabled region
- Physically separate power, cooling, and network infrastructure
- Synchronous replication for zone-redundant services

When to Use Availability Zones

- **Mission-critical apps** that must survive data center-level failures
- **Stateful workloads** that require zone-aware replication (e.g., SQL Managed Instances, Elasticsearch)
- **Load-balanced frontends** needing cross-zone distribution

Deployment Examples

Zone-redundant App Services

```
{
  "type": "Microsoft.Web/serverfarms",
  "apiVersion": "2021-02-01",
  "name": "[parameters('appServicePlanName')]",
  "location": "[resourceGroup().location]",
  "sku": {
    "name": "P1v3",
    "tier": "PremiumV3"
  },
  "properties": {
    "zoneRedundant": true
  }
}
```

Zonal AKS Cluster

Use `--zones 1 2 3` during creation to spread the nodes across three zones:

```
az aks create \
  --resource-group rg \
  --name aks-cluster \
  --node-count 3 \
  --zones 1 2 3
```

This ensures high resilience at the compute layer.

Region Pairs: Geo-Redundancy and Disaster Recovery

Each Azure region is paired with another region in the same geography to support disaster recovery. These **region pairs** are logically paired to allow:

- Data replication for services like Storage and SQL

- Automatic failover during service updates or major outages

- Geo-redundant backups and disaster recovery strategies

Examples:

- East US ↔ West US

- North Europe ↔ West Europe

- Southeast Asia ↔ East Asia

Architects use these pairs to:

- Deploy **active-passive** applications with failover

- Backup workloads using **GEO-redundant storage (GRS)**

- Implement **Azure Site Recovery** across paired regions

High Availability Through Redundancy Models

Azure offers multiple redundancy models depending on the service. Architects must choose based on workload criticality and cost.

Redundancy Model	Description	Example Services

Local Redundant (LRS)		Replicates data within a single zone	Azure Blob Storage, Disk Storage
Zone Redundant (ZRS)		Replicates data across zones	Azure Storage, App Services
Geo-Redundant (GRS)		LRS + async replication to paired region	Azure Blob Storage
Geo-Zone-Redundant		ZRS + geo-replication	Premium tiers of some services

Architectural choice depends on the balance between **RTO/RPO targets** and **budget constraints**.

Service Level Agreements (SLAs): What You Can Promise

SLAs define Azure's official uptime guarantee for services. It's critical that architects understand these commitments because they affect what the **business can promise** to customers.

Examples of Azure SLAs:

Service	SLA
App Service (Standard+)	99.95%
Azure Kubernetes Service	99.95% with multi-zone
Azure SQL Database	Up to 99.995%
Azure Front Door	99.99%
Storage (ZRS)	99.999999999% durability

Key implications:

- A 99.95% SLA allows for ~22 minutes of downtime/month.
- To improve uptime, combine services in HA configurations (e.g., multi-region).

Composite SLA Calculation

When multiple services are used together, the **effective SLA** is the product of each:

If Service A = 99.95%, and Service B = 99.9%, then:

```
Composite SLA = 0.9995 * 0.999 = 0.9985 = 99.85%
```

Architects must assess this risk and introduce redundancy or retries to mitigate potential failure points.

Architecting for Latency and Throughput

Latency directly affects user experience, especially in global apps. Azure provides several tools to optimize latency:

- **Azure Front Door**: Routes traffic to the nearest healthy backend.

- **Content Delivery Network (CDN)**: Caches content closer to users.

- **Traffic Manager**: DNS-based global traffic distribution.

- **Read replicas and geo-distributed databases**: e.g., Cosmos DB, Azure SQL Geo-replication.

Example scenario:

- Global e-commerce platform

- Front Door with App Services in East US, West Europe, and Southeast Asia

- Cosmos DB configured for multi-region writes

This architecture minimizes latency for users while preserving consistency and performance.

Testing Regional Failures

True resilience can only be validated through testing. Architects must design chaos experiments:

- Simulate zone failures using `az vm deallocate` or availability testing tools

- Disable Front Door backends and observe failover

- Force storage failover with GRS-enabled accounts (note: only in specific configurations)

Use **Azure Chaos Studio** for controlled fault injection:

```
az chaos experiment create \
  --name chaosTest \
  --resource-group rg \
  --location eastus \
  --target-resource-id
/subscriptions/.../resourceGroups/.../providers/Microsoft.Compute/vi
rtualMachines/myvm
```

These practices ensure the application can withstand real-world regional outages.

Regulatory and Compliance Considerations

For many industries, **where** your data lives is governed by law. Azure supports compliance with:

• **GDPR**:	Data	residency	in		Europe
• **HIPAA**:	Health	data	in	the	U.S.
• **FedRAMP**:	U.S.	federal	government		workloads
• **IRAP**:		Australian			government
• **Financial**	**Conduct**	**Authority**	**(FCA)** for	UK	finance

Architects must design region selection, backup, and data flows to avoid cross-border violations. Use **Customer Lockbox**, **Data Classification**, and **Compliance Manager** to enhance posture.

Conclusion

Selecting the right Azure regions and redundancy strategies is one of the most impactful decisions in cloud architecture. It affects performance, compliance, uptime, and customer trust. Availability Zones provide intra-region resilience, while region pairs enable geo-redundant disaster recovery.

Understanding the nuances of SLAs, latency management, redundancy models, and compliance ensures that architects can design solutions that not only scale, but also endure. In the next section, we'll explore how identity, subscription boundaries, and resource group design complete this foundation.

Subscription, Resource Group, and Identity Design

Effective architecture in Azure doesn't begin with a workload—it begins with **boundaries**. Before you deploy a single resource, you must carefully consider how your Azure environment will be structured in terms of **subscriptions, resource groups**, and **identity**. These foundational elements determine not only how your environment is governed and secured, but also how it scales, how teams collaborate, and how compliance and billing are managed across the enterprise.

A poor initial structure often leads to tangled permissions, limited scalability, unexpected cost spikes, and even security risks. This section will guide you through the architectural principles and best practices for structuring subscriptions, grouping resources, and designing identity models that support long-term growth and governance.

Azure Subscriptions: Strategic Partitioning

A **subscription** in Azure is a logical container for billing, access control, and resource deployment. All resources are deployed into a subscription, and every subscription is associated with a single Azure Active Directory (Azure AD) tenant.

Why Use Multiple Subscriptions?

Although a single subscription can host many resources, enterprises typically segment their workloads across **multiple subscriptions** to achieve:

- **Management boundary**: Separate dev, test, prod environments.

- **Delegated administration**: Assign teams full control of their own subscriptions.

- **Quota separation**: Avoid hitting resource limits like vCPU quotas or storage account caps.

- **Cost segregation**: Track billing per department or application.

- **Isolation and compliance**: Physically and logically isolate sensitive workloads.

Common Subscription Models

1. **Environment-based**:

   - Separate subscriptions for Development, QA, Staging, and Production.

   - Clear isolation, easier to manage policies and role assignments.

2. **Department-based**:

   - Subscriptions per business unit or function (e.g., Finance, HR, IT).

   - Supports showback and chargeback models.

3. **Application-based**:

   - Subscriptions dedicated to individual products or customer-facing services.

   - Ideal for microservices or distributed SaaS platforms.

Architects often combine these models to tailor solutions. For example, "Finance-Prod" and "Finance-Dev" subscriptions can coexist under a department and environment-based hybrid approach.

Subscription Governance via Management Groups

To manage multiple subscriptions at scale, Azure provides **Management Groups**, which allow you to:

- Apply **Azure Policy** and **Role-Based Access Control (RBAC)** across subscriptions.

- Inherit compliance and governance hierarchies.

- Align to corporate org charts or IT service boundaries.

Example hierarchy:

```
/ (Root Management Group)
├── Corp
│   ├── HR
│   │   ├── HR-Dev-Sub
│   │   └── HR-Prod-Sub
│   └── Finance
│       ├── Fin-Dev-Sub
│       └── Fin-Prod-Sub
```

Policy inheritance flows downward. If you assign a policy at the **Finance** management group level, it automatically applies to both subscriptions beneath it.

Resource Groups: Logical Organization

Within a subscription, resources are grouped into **Resource Groups (RGs)**. An RG is a container that holds related Azure resources, enabling them to be managed as a unit.

Best Practices for Resource Groups

- **Group by lifecycle**: Place resources that are deployed, updated, and deleted together into the same RG.

- **Don't group by type**: Avoid placing all VMs in one RG, all storage in another. This complicates lifecycle and access management.

- **Enable tagging**: Use tags like `environment`, `owner`, `costCenter`, `application` for cost management and governance.

- **Limit scope**: Keep RGs small enough to manage easily but large enough to group meaningful workloads.

Example of a resource group setup:

```
RG: App-Frontend-Prod
- App Service
- Azure CDN
- Front Door

RG: App-Backend-Prod
- Azure Functions
- Cosmos DB
- Key Vault
```

This separates deployment concerns while maintaining logical boundaries for development and operations.

Automation and Infrastructure as Code (IaC)

Resource Groups are often defined declaratively using Bicep, ARM, or Terraform:

```
resource rg 'Microsoft.Resources/resourceGroups@2021-04-01' = {
  name: 'finance-prod-backend'
  location: 'eastus'
}
```

IaC tools enforce consistency, reduce human error, and make rollbacks or audits much easier.

Identity and Access Management (IAM)

Identity is central to any Azure architecture. Azure uses **Azure Active Directory (AAD)** to manage identity and **Role-Based Access Control (RBAC)** to assign permissions.

Azure AD Tenants

Each organization typically has one Azure AD tenant, which can manage multiple subscriptions. Architects must align tenant strategy with:

- **User identity management**: Internal employees vs. external partners

- **Application identity**: Managed identities vs. app registrations

- **Multi-tenancy**: SaaS apps with isolated tenant experiences

Role-Based Access Control (RBAC)

RBAC assigns permissions to **users**, **groups**, **service principals**, or **managed identities** at different scopes:

- Management   group

- Subscription

- Resource   group

- Individual   resource

Azure provides **built-in roles** like `Owner`, `Contributor`, `Reader`, and **service-specific roles** like `SQL DB Contributor`, but you can also define **custom roles**.

```
{
  "Name": "Key Vault Reader",
  "IsCustom": true,
  "Actions": [
    "Microsoft.KeyVault/vaults/read",
    "Microsoft.KeyVault/vaults/secrets/list"
  ],
  "NotActions": [],
  "AssignableScopes": ["/subscriptions/{subscriptionId}"]
}
```

Use RBAC best practices:

- Apply   least-privilege   principle.

- Use **AAD groups** for assignments instead of individuals.

- Avoid assigning permissions at the individual resource level unless necessary.

- Use **Privileged Identity Management (PIM)** for time-bound admin access.

Managed Identities

Managed Identities allow Azure resources to securely authenticate with other services without storing credentials. There are two types:

- **System-assigned**: Tied to the lifecycle of a resource.

- **User-assigned**: Can be shared across multiple resources.

Use cases:

- A VM pulling secrets from Azure Key Vault

- An Azure Function writing logs to Azure Monitor

- AKS pods accessing Cosmos DB without a connection string

```
{
  "type": "Microsoft.ManagedIdentity/userAssignedIdentities",
  "name": "logging-identity",
  "location": "eastus"
}
```

Combined with policies, Managed Identities form the backbone of **secure automation** and **compliance-ready** services.

Policy and Governance

Azure Policy allows architects to enforce rules and conventions at scale. For example:

- Restrict VM SKUs to only cost-effective types

- Enforce tagging on all deployed resources

- Block public IPs on storage accounts

These policies can be assigned at the management group, subscription, or resource group level.

Example policy to enforce tags:

```
{
```

```
  "properties": {
    "displayName": "Require cost center tag",
    "policyRule": {
      "if": {
        "field": "tags['costCenter']",
        "exists": "false"
      },
      "then": {
        "effect": "deny"
      }
    }
  }
}
```

For scalable governance, combine policies with **Azure Blueprints** to define repeatable environments.

Cost Management and Showback

Subscriptions and resource groups should align with financial management objectives. Azure provides tools like:

- **Cost Analysis**: Visualize cost per resource or tag.
- **Budgets**: Define and alert on monthly spend thresholds.
- **Exports**: Automate billing data to storage for analysis.
- **Azure Cost Management + Billing**: Track usage and apply showback to teams.

Architects should encourage tagging consistency across all resources:

Tag Key	Description
environment	dev, test, staging, prod
owner	email or AD group
costCenter	Financial tracking for departments
application	Application or service identifier

Tenant and Subscription Security

Security architecture begins with **identity hardening**:

- **Enable MFA** for all users.

- Use **Conditional Access** to restrict login conditions.

- **Limit global admin roles** and monitor activity with **Azure AD Logs**.

- Regularly review RBAC assignments and rotate credentials for app registrations.

Cross-Tenant Scenarios

Some enterprises operate multiple tenants due to mergers or regional policies. In such cases:

- Use **Azure Lighthouse** to manage subscriptions across tenants securely.

- Implement **B2B collaboration** with custom domain branding and access policies.

- Ensure identity federation is established across tenants if SSO is required.

Conclusion

Subscription, resource group, and identity design are not administrative details—they are the **skeleton** of any Azure environment. They dictate how workloads scale, how teams operate, and how securely data flows.

By defining clear boundaries, applying identity best practices, and enforcing policy-driven governance, architects ensure their Azure platforms are not only robust and compliant, but ready for future innovation and expansion.

The next chapter will explore how to build on this foundation with scalable compute solutions, assessing trade-offs between VMs, App Services, and containers in real-world cloud architectures.

Chapter 3: Designing Scalable Compute Solutions

Virtual Machines vs. App Services vs. Azure Kubernetes Service

In the world of cloud architecture, **compute** is the core engine that powers applications. On Azure, architects have a broad range of compute options to choose from, each tailored to different workloads, scalability needs, and operational preferences. Understanding the trade-offs between **Virtual Machines (VMs)**, **App Services**, and **Azure Kubernetes Service (AKS)** is essential for making informed decisions that align with both technical and business goals.

This section explores these compute paradigms in-depth, comparing their capabilities, strengths, weaknesses, and best-fit scenarios. It also covers deployment patterns, scalability models, operational requirements, and architectural considerations for enterprise-grade solutions.

Virtual Machines (VMs)

Azure Virtual Machines provide Infrastructure-as-a-Service (IaaS) capabilities, offering the most control over the operating system and application environment.

Use Cases

- Legacy application lift-and-shift

- Custom runtime environments

- Applications requiring access to kernel-level features or specific OS configurations

- Traditional enterprise workloads such as SAP or SQL Server with failover clustering

Characteristics

- Full control of the OS, networking, disk configurations, and installed software

- Supports Windows, Linux, and custom images via Azure Image Gallery

- Requires manual management of patches, security updates, and scaling logic

Scalability

VMs can be scaled vertically (increase VM size) or horizontally (add more instances).

To achieve high availability and scalability:

- Use **Availability Sets** to protect against rack-level failures

- Use **Availability Zones** to protect against datacenter-level failures

- Use **Virtual Machine Scale Sets (VMSS)** to automatically scale VMs

Example: VMSS with autoscaling policy

```
resource scaleSet 'Microsoft.Compute/virtualMachineScaleSets@2023-
03-01' = {
  name: 'web-scale-set'
  location: resourceGroup().location
  sku: {
    name: 'Standard_D2s_v3'
    capacity: 3
  }
  properties: {
    upgradePolicy: {
      mode: 'Automatic'
    }
    virtualMachineProfile: {
      osProfile: {
        computerNamePrefix: 'webvm'
        adminUsername: 'azureuser'
      }
      storageProfile: {
        imageReference: {
          publisher: 'Canonical'
          offer: 'UbuntuServer'
          sku: '18.04-LTS'
          version: 'latest'
        }
        osDisk: {
          createOption: 'FromImage'
        }
      }
      networkProfile: {
        networkInterfaceConfigurations: [{
          name: 'nic'
          properties: {
```

```
          primary: true
          ipConfigurations: [{
            name: 'ipconfig'
            properties: {
              subnet: {
                id: subnet.id
              }
            }
          }]
        }
      }]
    }
  }
}
}
```

Pros

- Maximum   flexibility   and   control
- Ideal   for   specialized   workloads   or   custom   configurations
- Integrates   well   with   existing   on-prem   infrastructure

Cons

- Higher   operational   overhead
- Manual   patching   and   OS   maintenance
- Slower   to   deploy   and   scale   compared   to   PaaS   options

Azure App Services

Azure App Service is a Platform-as-a-Service (PaaS) offering designed for hosting web applications, REST APIs, and mobile backends with minimal infrastructure management.

Use Cases

- Web   apps   and   websites
- RESTful   APIs

- Backend services for mobile or SPA apps

- Fast development and deployment environments

Characteristics

- Supports .NET, Node.js, Java, Python, PHP, and custom containers

- Built-in DevOps integration with GitHub Actions and Azure DevOps

- Horizontal autoscaling, deployment slots, staging environments

Scalability

App Services automatically scale horizontally based on metrics like CPU usage, memory, or HTTP queue length. You can configure autoscale rules manually or use the default behavior with a Premium App Service Plan.

Example autoscale rule with ARM:

```json
{
  "type": "Microsoft.Insights/autoscalesettings",
  "name": "autoscale-appservice",
  "properties": {
    "targetResourceUri":            "[resourceId('Microsoft.Web/sites',
parameters('appName'))]",
    "enabled": true,
    "profiles": [
      {
        "name": "default",
        "capacity": {
          "minimum": "1",
          "maximum": "10",
          "default": "2"
        },
        "rules": [
          {
            "metricTrigger": {
              "metricName": "CpuPercentage",
              "timeGrain": "PT1M",
              "statistic": "Average",
              "timeWindow": "PT5M",
              "timeAggregation": "Average",
```

```
          "operator": "GreaterThan",
          "threshold": 70
        },
        "scaleAction": {
          "direction": "Increase",
          "type": "ChangeCount",
          "value": "1",
          "cooldown": "PT1M"
        }
      }
    ]
  }
]
}
}
```

Pros

- Rapid deployment and simplified management
- Built-in features like SSL, custom domains, backups, scaling
- Integrated identity, security, and VNET connectivity

Cons

- Limited OS and configuration control
- Not suitable for apps needing kernel-level access
- Less suitable for high-throughput microservices compared to AKS

Azure Kubernetes Service (AKS)

AKS is Azure's managed Kubernetes platform, offering full container orchestration, auto-scaling, service discovery, and integration with CI/CD pipelines.

Use Cases

- Microservice architectures
- Containerized applications with complex dependencies

- Multitenant SaaS platforms with isolation requirements
- Event-driven and real-time systems

Characteristics

- Full Kubernetes API access
- Node pools with different VM SKUs
- Integration with Azure Monitor, Azure Policy, AAD, Azure Files/Disks
- Can run both Windows and Linux containers

Scalability

AKS supports both:

- **Cluster autoscaler**: Adds/removes nodes based on demand
- **Horizontal Pod Autoscaler (HPA)**: Scales pods based on CPU/memory/custom metrics

Example HPA configuration in YAML:

```yaml
apiVersion: autoscaling/v2
kind: HorizontalPodAutoscaler
metadata:
  name: backend-api-hpa
spec:
  scaleTargetRef:
    apiVersion: apps/v1
    kind: Deployment
    name: backend-api
  minReplicas: 2
  maxReplicas: 10
  metrics:
    - type: Resource
      resource:
        name: cpu
        target:
          type: Utilization
          averageUtilization: 60
```

Pros

- Full control over containers and orchestration
- Ideal for complex deployments and high scale
- Flexible CI/CD and DevOps tooling

Cons

- Steeper learning curve
- More operational overhead than App Services
- Security and upgrade responsibility lies with the team

Comparison Table

Feature	Virtual Machines	App Service	Azure Kubernetes Service
Abstraction Level	IaaS	PaaS	CaaS / Container Orchestration
OS Control	Full	Limited	Full inside containers
Deployment Speed	Slower	Fast	Moderate
Scaling Type	Manual / VMSS	Auto (horizontal)	Auto (pod/node)
DevOps Integration	Manual	Built-in	Custom via pipelines
Ideal For	Legacy / Custom workloads	Web/API apps	Microservices / Event-driven
Cost Efficiency	Low (overhead)	High	High (at scale)
Learning Curve	Moderate	Low	High

Decision Criteria for Architects

When deciding between these options, architects must evaluate based on:

- **Control vs. Productivity**: Do you need fine-grained control or rapid deployment?

- **Team Maturity**: Does the team have the expertise for container orchestration?

- **Scalability Needs**: Will the app need to handle spikes in traffic or continuous growth?

- **Operational Model**: Are you prepared to manage patches, upgrades, and security?

- **Cost Model**: Can you optimize the service for long-running vs. bursty workloads?

Hybrid Approaches

Many enterprise architectures combine these services:

- Use **App Service** for frontend or user-facing APIs.

- Use **AKS** for backend processing and microservices.

- Use **VMs** for legacy workloads or domain-specific components like Active Directory, file shares, or third-party agents.

This allows you to balance innovation with risk mitigation and accommodate both legacy and cloud-native paradigms.

Conclusion

Each compute model in Azure serves a distinct purpose, and the best architectures often mix and match based on application characteristics, team capability, and business goals. Virtual Machines offer maximum control but demand more maintenance. App Services simplify web and API hosting with minimal ops. AKS provides the power and flexibility of Kubernetes for microservices and high-scale systems.

The role of the Azure Architect is to evaluate these options holistically and implement scalable, maintainable, and secure compute layers that evolve alongside the organization's cloud journey. In the next section, we'll explore the strategies for autoscaling these compute environments and ensuring they can meet changing demand in real-time.

Auto-scaling Strategies and Patterns

Auto-scaling is one of the most powerful advantages of cloud computing. It allows systems to automatically adjust capacity based on demand, ensuring high performance while optimizing cost. In Azure, auto-scaling is available across various compute services including Virtual

Machines, App Services, Azure Kubernetes Service (AKS), Azure Functions, and more. However, successful auto-scaling isn't just about enabling a toggle—it requires thoughtful design, monitoring, metric selection, and fault-tolerant patterns.

This section explores auto-scaling strategies across Azure's core compute platforms, outlines scaling patterns, and offers guidance on monitoring and testing scale behavior to meet both technical and business objectives.

The Purpose of Auto-scaling

Auto-scaling exists to serve three primary objectives:

1. **Maintain performance and reliability** during varying workloads.

2. **Optimize cost** by releasing unused resources when demand drops.

3. **Improve availability** and resiliency in response to failures or traffic surges.

Architects must design for all three simultaneously, accounting for workload behavior, concurrency limits, cold starts, and scaling latency.

Reactive vs. Predictive Scaling

Auto-scaling strategies generally fall into two categories:

Reactive Scaling

- Adjusts resources in real-time based on current metrics.

- Most commonly used in Azure (e.g., CPU threshold on App Services).

- Examples: VMSS increasing instance count when CPU > 80%, AKS pod scale-up when memory > 70%.

Predictive Scaling

- Uses historical patterns to proactively scale ahead of demand.

- Useful for predictable workloads like daily ETL jobs, nightly batch processes, or business hours traffic.

- Can be implemented using Azure Automation, scheduled scaling rules, or machine learning models.

Hybrid strategies are ideal—combine scheduled scaling for baseline capacity and reactive rules for unanticipated spikes.

Auto-scaling on Azure Virtual Machine Scale Sets (VMSS)

VMSS enables horizontal scaling of VMs under a shared configuration and load balancer.

Key Features:

- Supports autoscale rules based on metrics like CPU, memory, disk IO, or custom metrics via Azure Monitor.

- Custom images and script extensions are supported.

- Works with Availability Zones and Load Balancer for resiliency.

Example ARM autoscale rule for VMSS:

```json
{
  "type": "Microsoft.Insights/autoscalesettings",
  "name": "autoscale-vmss",
  "properties": {
    "targetResourceUri":
"[resourceId('Microsoft.Compute/virtualMachineScaleSets',    'web-
vmss')]",
    "enabled": true,
    "profiles": [
      {
        "name": "scale-out",
        "capacity": {
          "minimum": "2",
          "maximum": "10",
          "default": "3"
        },
        "rules": [
          {
            "metricTrigger": {
              "metricName": "Percentage CPU",
              "timeGrain": "PT1M",
              "statistic": "Average",
              "timeWindow": "PT5M",
              "timeAggregation": "Average",
              "operator": "GreaterThan",
              "threshold": 75
            },
            "scaleAction": {
```

```
            "direction": "Increase",
            "type": "ChangeCount",
            "value": "1",
            "cooldown": "PT5M"
          }
        }
      ]
    }
  ]
}
}
```

Considerations:

- Scaling actions take time to provision new VMs.

- Use health probes and warm-up scripts to avoid sending traffic to under-prepared nodes.

- Combine with Azure Load Balancer for even traffic distribution.

Auto-scaling on Azure App Services

App Services support horizontal scaling across multiple instances based on a wide range of metrics:

- CPU   Percentage

- Memory   Usage

- HTTP   Queue   Length

- Request   Count

- Custom   Metrics   (via   Azure   Monitor)

Auto-scaling Mechanisms:

- Manual   Scale: Fixed   number   of   instances

- Rule-based   Auto-scale: Based   on   thresholds

- Scheduled   Auto-scale: Fixed   capacity   at   specific   times

Example use case: A retail site experiences heavy traffic on weekends. You can configure scheduled scale-up rules for Friday 6 PM through Sunday night, and reactive CPU-based rules for all other times.

Best Practices:

- Use deployment slots to manage scale safely with zero downtime deployments.

- Monitor **cold start latency** when scaling up from zero.

- Use App Service Environment (ASE) for isolated scale at enterprise level.

Auto-scaling in Azure Kubernetes Service (AKS)

AKS supports two main scaling dimensions:

Cluster Autoscaler

- Scales **nodes** in a node pool.

- Triggers when pods cannot be scheduled due to insufficient resources.

- Requires enabling autoscaler via `az aks update`.

```
az aks update \
  --resource-group rg \
  --name aks-cluster \
  --enable-cluster-autoscaler \
  --min-count 2 \
  --max-count 10
```

Horizontal Pod Autoscaler (HPA)

- Scales **pods** in a deployment based on CPU, memory, or custom metrics.

HPA example in YAML:

```
apiVersion: autoscaling/v2
kind: HorizontalPodAutoscaler
metadata:
  name: api-hpa
spec:
  scaleTargetRef:
```

```
apiVersion: apps/v1
kind: Deployment
name: api-service
minReplicas: 3
maxReplicas: 10
metrics:
  - type: Resource
    resource:
      name: cpu
      target:
        type: Utilization
        averageUtilization: 65
```

Advanced Scaling Patterns:

- Use **KEDA (Kubernetes Event-driven Autoscaling)** for scaling based on queues, events, or custom metrics.

- Use **multiple node pools** for specialized workloads (GPU, memory-heavy).

Challenges:

- Scaling latency when provisioning new nodes

- Complex cost management

- Require deep monitoring to tune thresholds correctly

Auto-scaling with Azure Functions

Azure Functions scale **serverlessly**, meaning there's no infrastructure to manage. Scaling is triggered by:

- Number of incoming events (HTTP, queues, blobs, Event Hub, etc.)

- Concurrency settings

- Plan type (Consumption, Premium, Dedicated)

Plan Types:

- **Consumption Plan**: Auto-scales from 0; ideal for event-driven bursty workloads.

- **Premium Plan**: Offers VNET integration, warm-up instances, and scaling rules.

- **Dedicated App Service Plan**: Manual control of instance count.

Consumption Plan sample:

```json
{
  "bindings": [
    {
      "name": "queueItem",
      "type": "queueTrigger",
      "direction": "in",
      "queueName": "orders",
      "connection": "AzureWebJobsStorage"
    }
  ]
}
```

When messages arrive in the queue, Azure automatically spins up instances to process them in parallel.

Considerations:

- Cold start latency for HTTP-triggered functions in Consumption Plan

- Use Premium Plan or pre-warmed instances for low-latency APIs

- Implement **idempotency** and **retry logic** for safe scale-out

Monitoring and Tuning Auto-scaling

Without observability, auto-scaling becomes guesswork. Azure Monitor and Application Insights offer real-time metrics and historical data to fine-tune scaling policies.

Key Metrics to Track:

- CPU, memory, disk I/O

- Queue length, request count

- Response time and error rates

- Pod unscheduled count (AKS)

- Cold starts and time to warm (Functions)

Tools:

- **Azure Monitor Metrics Explorer**: Graphs and alerts
- **Workbooks**: Visualize complex metrics across services
- **Log Analytics**: Write KQL queries for trend analysis

KQL query example for CPU usage:

```
Perf
| where ObjectName == "Processor"
| summarize avg(CounterValue) by bin(TimeGenerated, 5m), Computer
```

Set alerts on metrics to be notified of under or over-scaling events.

Patterns and Anti-patterns

Effective Patterns:

- **Buffer-based scaling**: Scale based on queue length or backlog (common in retail, banking).

- **Scheduled + Reactive Hybrid**: Combine forecasted traffic and real-time metrics.

- **Graceful scaling**: Use **pre-warming**, **cool-down periods**, and **lifecycle hooks**.

Anti-patterns:

- Scaling on unstable metrics (e.g., request count spikes without duration consideration).

- Aggressive scale-in that terminates instances mid-processing.

- Ignoring warm-up time, leading to temporary failures.

- No cap on scale-out, risking cost explosion.

Cost Optimization and Limits

Auto-scaling introduces dynamic billing. Without safeguards, costs can spiral unexpectedly.

Tips:

- Define **min/max** **instance** **limits**.

- Use **budgets** and **alerts** for cost thresholds.

- Offload static content to CDN to reduce backend pressure.

- Use **spot instances** for stateless or interruptible tasks (e.g., image processing).

Testing Auto-scaling Behavior

To validate scaling logic:

- Use **load testing tools** (e.g., Azure Load Testing, Apache JMeter)

- Simulate queue bursts for serverless systems

- Create synthetic users and sessions for web apps

- Use **Azure Chaos Studio** to test resiliency during scale operations

Conclusion

Auto-scaling is a critical enabler of performance and cost-efficiency in modern cloud architecture. By choosing the right metrics, configuring scaling policies properly, and testing under load, architects can build resilient systems that respond to real-world demand with precision.

Each Azure compute platform—VMSS, App Services, AKS, Functions—offers unique scaling mechanisms. An architect's job is to understand these differences, align scaling strategies with application behavior, and ensure that the system can grow, shrink, and recover gracefully.

The next section will explore how to design applications that are inherently stateless and horizontally scalable—foundational traits for effective auto-scaling in cloud environments.

Stateless Design and Horizontal Scaling

In cloud-native architecture, **statelessness** is not just a design principle—it is a fundamental requirement for achieving **horizontal scalability**. Stateless applications are easier to scale, more resilient to failure, and better suited for distributed systems like microservices and serverless platforms. Designing your compute architecture to be stateless unlocks the ability to add or remove instances dynamically, distribute traffic efficiently, and recover gracefully from failure.

This section explores the core concepts, patterns, and implementation techniques for stateless application design in Azure. It also highlights the challenges of stateful systems and how to externalize state using services like Azure Cache for Redis, Azure Cosmos DB, Azure Storage, and durable messaging.

What Does Stateless Mean?

A **stateless** service does not retain information (state) about user sessions or transactions between requests. Each request contains all the information needed for the server to process it independently.

For example, a stateless API might process a purchase request using data included in the HTTP body or token, without storing intermediate steps on the server.

In contrast, a **stateful** system stores information between requests, such as user sessions, file uploads in progress, or application context.

Statelessness enables:

- Horizontal   scale-out

- Load   balancer-friendly   deployments

- Retry-safe   operations

- Simplified   failover   and   blue/green   deployments

Benefits of Stateless Design

1. **Elastic   Scalability**
   New instances can be spun up or down at any time without disrupting existing requests.

2. **Improved   Availability**
   Stateless services can easily reroute traffic to healthy nodes, supporting zone or region   failover.

3. **Simplified   Load   Balancing**
   Since every instance is interchangeable, traffic can be evenly distributed.

4. **Ease   of   Deployment**
   You can upgrade and deploy without worrying about in-flight sessions or affinity.

5. **Better   Cost   Efficiency**
   Idle   instances   can   be   terminated   without   risk   of   data   loss.

Common Stateless Application Patterns

RESTful APIs

Design APIs to be stateless by ensuring each call is complete and independent. Use JSON Web Tokens (JWT) to pass user identity and roles, avoiding server-side session storage.

Function-as-a-Service (FaaS)

Azure Functions in the Consumption Plan are inherently stateless. They start, execute, and terminate without any retained memory between invocations.

Microservices

Services that encapsulate specific business functions and interact via APIs or events should not depend on shared memory or sessions. Use message queues to pass context and state.

Externalizing State

The key to stateless design is **externalizing state**—moving session, configuration, and temporary data out of the application memory and into reliable, shared services.

Azure Cache for Redis

Use Redis to store temporary session state, counters, feature flags, or real-time metrics.

Example: Node.js storing a user session in Redis

```
const redis = require('redis');
const client = redis.createClient();
client.setex(`session:${userId}`,                           3600,
JSON.stringify(sessionData));
```

Redis is in-memory, highly performant, and supports automatic failover in Premium tiers.

Azure Cosmos DB

For persistent, high-scale state, use Cosmos DB. Partition your data by user ID, tenant ID, or another logical key to support horizontal scale.

Example: Partition key strategy

```
{
  "partitionKey": {
    "paths": ["/userId"],
    "kind": "Hash"
  }
}
```

This ensures data is distributed across nodes and avoids cross-partition throttling.

Azure Storage (Blob/Table/Queue)

- Store large objects (images, PDFs) in Blob Storage.

- Use Table Storage for NoSQL-style key-value access.

- Use Queues for asynchronous message handling.

External storage services are highly available and support geo-replication for resiliency.

Designing Stateless Web Applications

Avoid In-Memory Sessions

ASP.NET and other web frameworks often default to in-memory sessions, which tie users to specific servers (session affinity). This breaks scaling and failover.

Use **Redis-backed session providers** or pass session data via tokens:

```
services.AddStackExchangeRedisCache(options =>
{
    options.Configuration = Configuration["Redis:ConnectionString"];
});
services.AddSession(options =>
{
    options.IdleTimeout = TimeSpan.FromMinutes(30);
    options.Cookie.HttpOnly = true;
});
```

Decouple UI from Server State

Modern frontend frameworks like React, Angular, or Blazor WebAssembly should not rely on the backend to manage UI state. Instead, pass user state via JWT or fetch it on demand from APIs.

Use **Azure AD B2C** or **MSAL** to maintain stateless authentication flows.

Designing Stateless APIs

Key techniques:

- **Idempotency**: Ensure repeated API calls have the same effect. Use transaction IDs or request hashes.

- **Authentication Tokens**: Use JWTs or OAuth 2.0 tokens that include claims about the user, eliminating the need for server-side sessions.

- **Timeouts and Retries**: All downstream service calls should be wrapped in retry logic and timeouts to protect the caller.

Example retry pattern in Node.js:

```
async function retry(fn, retries = 3) {
  for (let i = 0; i < retries; i++) {
    try {
      return await fn();
    } catch (error) {
      if (i === retries - 1) throw error;
      await new Promise(res => setTimeout(res, 1000 * (i + 1)));
    }
  }
}
```

Stateless Microservices and Event-driven Architecture

Stateless services thrive in **event-driven** architectures where services communicate via messages or events instead of direct API calls.

Use **Azure Service Bus**, **Event Grid**, or **Event Hubs** to:

- Publish events like `OrderPlaced`, `UserRegistered`

- Trigger Azure Functions or microservices to process events

- Decouple producers and consumers

This architecture allows each component to be stateless and independently scalable.

Stateless Scaling on Azure

Azure makes it easy to scale stateless services:

- **Azure App Services**: Auto-scale by instance count

- **Azure Kubernetes Service (AKS)**: Scale pods based on CPU, memory, or custom metrics

- **Azure Functions**: Auto-scale based on trigger rate

- **VM Scale Sets**: Add/remove VMs without managing internal state

In all these scenarios, the key enabler is the statelessness of the application. Without internal state, instances can come and go as needed.

Managing Configuration in a Stateless World

Avoid storing configuration in application code or local files. Instead, use:

- **Azure App Configuration**: Centralized configuration store with feature flag support

- **Azure Key Vault**: Store secrets, connection strings, API keys

- **Environment Variables**: Use deployment scripts or IaC to inject settings into runtime environments

Example using environment variables in Bicep:

```
resource webapp 'Microsoft.Web/sites@2022-03-01' = {
  name: 'myapp'
  location: resourceGroup().location
  properties: {
    siteConfig: {
      appSettings: [
        {
          name: 'CosmosDbEndpoint'
          value: cosmosDb.properties.documentEndpoint
        }
      ]
    }
  }
}
```

This approach supports **immutable infrastructure** and **zero-downtime deployments**.

Testing and Observability in Stateless Applications

Stateless apps are easier to test because their output is purely a function of their inputs. However, they must still be observed closely.

Use:

- **Distributed Tracing** with Application Insights
- **Log Correlation** using trace IDs
- **Synthetic Transactions** to test APIs from multiple regions

Kusto Query Language (KQL) for tracing:

```
requests
| where operation_Name == "PlaceOrder"
| summarize avg(duration) by cloud_RoleInstance
```

This shows which instance is slowest, regardless of how many scale units are active.

Edge Cases: When You Must Be Stateful

Some applications inherently require stateful behavior:

- Multiplayer game sessions
- Real-time chat or streaming
- Long-running workflows

In such cases, minimize coupling by:

- Isolating stateful components
- Using Azure Durable Functions for orchestrations
- Persisting state to shared services (e.g., Cosmos DB, Azure SQL)

Summary Design Patterns

Pattern	Description
Stateless API with JWT	No server session; all auth in token
Cache-aside with Redis	Application checks Redis before DB
Event sourcing	Store events instead of current state

| CQRS | Separate read/write models with event replay |

| Function Chaining (Durable) | Stateless serverless chained via context |

Conclusion

Stateless design is a prerequisite for building highly scalable, resilient, and cost-efficient applications on Azure. By externalizing state, adopting idempotent practices, and leveraging cloud-native services like Azure Redis, Cosmos DB, and Key Vault, architects can build systems that scale horizontally with ease.

Horizontal scaling becomes trivial when no instance is unique or irreplaceable. Statelessness not only unlocks elasticity but also aligns with DevOps, containerization, and microservices—all of which are core to modern cloud architecture. In the next chapter, we will explore scalable storage strategies that complement these stateless systems and enable high-throughput, low-latency data access at global scale.

Chapter 4: Architecting Scalable Storage Solutions

Azure Storage Account Types and Use Cases

Storage is a foundational pillar of any cloud architecture, and in Azure, selecting the right type of storage is critical to performance, cost, durability, and scalability. Microsoft Azure offers a versatile set of storage services under the umbrella of **Azure Storage Accounts**, each tailored to specific data types, access patterns, and durability needs.

Understanding the various storage account types, their configurations, access methods, and use cases empowers architects to make informed decisions that align with both technical requirements and business constraints.

Overview of Azure Storage Account Types

An **Azure Storage Account** is a container for several types of storage services, including:

1. **Blob Storage** – Unstructured data like images, documents, backups, and logs.

2. **File Storage (Azure Files)** – Managed file shares using SMB/NFS protocols.

3. **Queue Storage** – Simple message queuing for communication between components.

4. **Table Storage** – NoSQL key-value store for structured, non-relational data.

5. **Disk Storage** – High-performance block storage for Azure VMs.

Depending on the storage needs, architects can choose from different storage account types:

Storage Account Type	Supports	Common Use Case
General-purpose v2 (GPv2)	Blobs, Files, Queues, Tables	Modern apps, broad workloads
Blob Storage	BlockBlob and AppendBlob only	Cost-optimized blob workloads
General-purpose v1 (GPv1)	All services but legacy performance	Legacy systems, price-sensitive needs

BlockBlobStorage	BlockBlob only, premium performance	Media, telemetry, big data
FileStorage	Premium Azure Files only	High IOPS SMB file shares

GPv2 accounts are recommended for most new workloads because they provide access to all modern features, including tiered blob storage, soft delete, lifecycle management, and hierarchical namespace (when enabled for ADLS Gen2).

Blob Storage: Core for Unstructured Data

Blob storage is Azure's object storage solution for unstructured data—ideal for images, videos, documents, backups, logs, and big data.

Blob types:

- **Block blobs**: Optimal for large files, supports parallel upload.

- **Append blobs**: Good for logging scenarios, where data is added sequentially.

- **Page blobs**: Used primarily for Azure VM disks.

Architectural use cases:

- Store media files for a web app.

- Host static websites.

- Offload backups from SQL/Azure Files.

- Store telemetry and log files for analysis.

Blob Tiers

To balance cost and performance, Azure supports multiple access tiers:

Tier	Optimized For	Typical Use Case
Hot	Frequent access	Web content, active data
Cool	Infrequent access (≥30d)	Backup data, archival logs

| Archive | Rare access (≥180d) | Legal compliance, old media |

Blob tiers can be set per blob and transitioned automatically via **Lifecycle Management Rules**.

Example lifecycle policy JSON:

```json
{
  "rules": [
    {
      "enabled": true,
      "name": "ArchiveOldData",
      "type": "Lifecycle",
      "definition": {
        "filters": {
          "blobTypes": ["blockBlob"],
          "prefixMatch": ["log/"]
        },
        "actions": {
          "baseBlob": {
            "tierToArchive": {
              "daysAfterModificationGreaterThan": 90
            },
            "delete": {
              "daysAfterModificationGreaterThan": 365
            }
          }
        }
      }
    }
  ]
}
```

Azure Files: Shared File System in the Cloud

Azure Files provides fully managed file shares accessible via **SMB** or **NFS**, making it an ideal option for lift-and-shift scenarios or applications requiring shared storage.

Key features:

- Mount on Windows, Linux, and macOS

- Azure File Sync for hybrid cloud deployments
- Active Directory authentication
- Zone-redundant and geo-redundant storage

Use cases:

- VDI environments storing user profiles
- Shared configuration and data between containers
- Replacing on-prem NAS systems

Pricing tiers:

- **Standard**: HDD-backed, best for general-purpose workloads.
- **Premium**: SSD-backed, high-throughput and low-latency.

Queue Storage: Lightweight Messaging

Azure Queue Storage provides a simple, reliable, and scalable message queue for decoupled application components.

Design advantages:

- Enables async processing for background jobs
- Durable message retention (up to 7 days by default, configurable)
- FIFO order supported with visibility timeouts

Use case example:

- A web app uploads user photos → adds queue message → background service resizes the image and stores the result.

Queue message example using Azure SDK (Node.js):

```
const { QueueClient } = require("@azure/storage-queue");
const queueClient = new QueueClient("<queue-connection-string>",
"resize-requests");
```

```
await queueClient.sendMessage(Buffer.from(JSON.stringify({ imageId:
"123" })).toString("base64"));
```

For more advanced messaging needs (e.g., pub-sub, sessions, deduplication), consider **Azure Service Bus**.

Table Storage: Simple NoSQL for Structured Data

Azure Table Storage is a highly scalable key-value store for structured NoSQL data.

Advantages:

- Massive scale (PBs)
- Fast read/write via partition keys
- Low-cost alternative to full database services

Use cases:

- IoT device metrics
- App telemetry
- Lightweight user metadata

Limitations:

- No relational features (joins, transactions)
- Indexing limited to PartitionKey and RowKey

For more complex scenarios, use **Cosmos DB with Table API**, which adds global distribution, automatic indexing, and enterprise-grade SLAs.

Disk Storage: Block Storage for Azure VMs

Azure Disk Storage provides persistent, high-performance storage for Azure Virtual Machines. These are block-level storage devices attached to VMs.

Types:

- **Standard HDD**: Cost-effective for infrequent access.

- **Standard SSD:** Balanced cost/performance.
- **Premium SSD:** High throughput and low latency.
- **Ultra Disk:** Custom performance tiers, ideal for databases.

Use cases:

- OS disks, data disks
- SQL Server, Oracle, SAP
- High-performance transactional systems

Attach disks declaratively in Bicep:

```
resource dataDisk 'Microsoft.Compute/disks@2022-03-02' = {
  name: 'myDataDisk'
  location: resourceGroup().location
  sku: {
    name: 'Premium_LRS'
  }
  properties: {
    creationData: {
      createOption: 'Empty'
    }
    diskSizeGB: 256
  }
}
```

Choosing the Right Storage Type

Requirement	Recommended Service	Azure
Unstructured data (media, backups)	Blob Storage	
Shared files across VMs/containers	Azure Files	
Asynchronous job processing	Queue Storage	

NoSQL key-value store	Table Storage or Cosmos DB
Persistent disks for VMs/databases	Azure Disk Storage

Key architectural considerations:

- **Durability**: All storage services offer at least 99.999999999% durability.

- **Latency**: Premium and Ultra tiers reduce latency for IOPS-intensive applications.

- **Cost**: Hot tier is more expensive than Cool or Archive; Premium Files cost more but deliver lower latency.

- **Scalability**: Blob and Table Storage scale almost infinitely; disks have size and throughput limits.

Resilience and Redundancy Options

Azure provides multiple redundancy options across its storage services:

Redundancy Type	Scope	Use Case
LRS (Locally Redundant)	Single datacenter	Cost-effective local protection
ZRS (Zone Redundant)	Across availability zones	High availability in a region
GRS (Geo Redundant)	Across paired regions	Disaster recovery
RA-GRS	GRS + read access	Read optimization + resilience

Example of selecting ZRS in ARM:

```
{
  "sku": {
    "name": "Standard_ZRS"
  },
  "kind": "StorageV2",
  "properties": {
    "accessTier": "Hot"
  }
}
```

Choose redundancy based on SLA requirements, cost constraints, and regulatory needs.

Monitoring and Security

Monitoring:

- **Azure Monitor** integrates with storage accounts to emit metrics (requests, egress, latency).

- **Diagnostic Settings** can stream logs to Log Analytics or Event Hub.

Security:

- Use **Azure RBAC** for granular access control.

- Enable **private endpoints** to restrict access over internal VNet.

- Use **Azure Key Vault** to manage encryption keys (customer-managed keys, CMK).

- Enable **Advanced Threat Protection** for storage accounts to detect suspicious activity.

Conclusion

Azure's storage services are diverse, powerful, and engineered for global scale. Selecting the right type of storage account and service can dramatically influence application performance, scalability, availability, and cost efficiency.

By understanding when and how to use Blob Storage, Azure Files, Queues, Tables, and Disks, architects can compose robust storage strategies that support every kind of workload—from simple static file hosting to mission-critical transactional systems. In the next section, we'll dive into how to partition and shard this storage to meet scale and throughput requirements as your application grows.

Data Partitioning and Sharding Techniques

As applications grow in scale and complexity, managing massive volumes of data becomes a critical architectural challenge. Traditional storage approaches quickly hit performance, availability, and scalability limits when forced to handle large, concurrent workloads. To overcome these constraints, architects rely on **data partitioning** and **sharding**—strategies that divide large datasets into smaller, more manageable parts that can be distributed across multiple storage units or compute nodes.

In Azure, partitioning and sharding are foundational to building storage systems that scale predictably, perform reliably under load, and remain cost-effective over time. This section explores core partitioning and sharding concepts, design patterns, and implementation techniques across Azure storage services, databases, and distributed systems.

Understanding Partitioning and Sharding

While the terms are often used interchangeably, **partitioning** and **sharding** are distinct but related concepts:

- **Partitioning** refers to dividing data within a single data store into separate logical units (partitions) to enable parallelism and performance.

- **Sharding** is a form of horizontal partitioning where data is split across multiple **physical** databases, containers, or services, often distributed geographically or across clusters.

In practice:

- Partitioning = logical separation within one storage system

- Sharding = distributing across many storage systems

Both techniques aim to reduce contention, improve throughput, and isolate failure domains.

Benefits of Partitioning and Sharding

1. **Scalability**: Enables systems to grow linearly by spreading load across nodes or containers.

2. **Performance**: Reduces read/write contention and increases parallelism.

3. **Availability**: Allows individual partitions or shards to fail or be updated independently.

4. **Cost Optimization**: Enables targeted resource allocation to high-demand data segments.

5. **Data Isolation**: Critical for multi-tenant SaaS platforms and regulatory compliance.

Partitioning in Azure Storage and Cosmos DB

Azure Blob Storage

Blob storage uses **partition keys** behind the scenes. The performance of operations depends on how blobs are named—especially the prefix.

Key Design Tip: Avoid sequential naming (e.g., `log1.txt`, `log2.txt`). This creates a hotspot on a single partition. Instead, use prefixes based on GUIDs, timestamps, or hash functions.

Example blob names:

- ✗   `logs/2023-01-01/01.txt`,   `logs/2023-01-01/02.txt`

- ✓   `logs/2023-01-01/a4f9-01.txt`,   `logs/2023-01-01/b3f2-02.txt`

Azure Storage automatically rebalances partitions, but distributing load early improves scale.

Azure Cosmos DB

Cosmos DB explicitly supports **logical partitioning**, which is essential for achieving performance at scale.

Each item in a container is associated with a **partition key**, and the database engine distributes data across logical partitions.

Example partition key definition (Bicep):

```
resource                                                        cosmosContainer
'Microsoft.DocumentDB/databaseAccounts/sqlDatabases/containers@2021-
06-15' = {
  name: 'ordersdb/orders/transactions'
  properties: {
    partitionKey: {
      paths: ['/customerId']
      kind: 'Hash'
    }
  }
}
```

Best Practices for Cosmos DB Partitioning

1. **High cardinality**: Choose a key with many unique values to evenly distribute data.

2. **Even access patterns**: Select a key that is queried frequently and consistently.

3. **Avoid "hot partitions"**: Don't use keys that skew traffic, like `region` or `tenantId` if one dominates.

4. **Small partition size**: Keep partitions under 20GB for best performance.

A bad partition key can cripple performance. For example, using `orderStatus` (e.g., "pending", "shipped") will result in a few massive partitions, degrading throughput.

Sharding Patterns in Azure SQL and PostgreSQL

Sharding becomes necessary when partitioning within a single database isn't enough, especially for multi-tenant applications or high-scale transactional systems.

Azure SQL Database

Azure SQL does not offer native sharding, so architects must implement it manually or use **Elastic Database Tools**.

Sharding techniques:

- **Vertical Sharding**: Divide tables by function (e.g., users in one DB, orders in another).

- **Horizontal Sharding**: Divide rows by key (e.g., customer ID range).

Example horizontal shard strategy:

- Shard 1: CustomerID 1–10,000 → `sql-db-shard1`

- Shard 2: CustomerID 10,001–20,000 → `sql-db-shard2`

- Routing logic in middleware/service layer

Elastic Database Query enables cross-shard querying using T-SQL:

```
SELECT * FROM Orders
WHERE CustomerID = 12345
```

Azure SQL routes the query to the appropriate shard via a shard map manager.

Azure Database for PostgreSQL (Flexible Server)

Sharding in PostgreSQL is usually handled via application logic or tools like **Citus**, which is available as a managed service via **Azure Cosmos DB for PostgreSQL**.

Use `CREATE DISTRIBUTED TABLE` for sharded tables:

```
SELECT create_distributed_table('orders', 'customer_id');
```

Citus shards data by `customer_id` and distributes it across worker nodes.

Benefits:

- Transparent   scaling

- High   concurrency

- Global   distribution   with   region-based   workers

Sharding in NoSQL and Distributed Systems

Table Storage

Azure Table Storage does not allow explicit partition key configuration, but like Cosmos DB, it benefits from thoughtful design of the `PartitionKey` and `RowKey`.

Key Design Goal	Strategy
Maximize performance	Use high-cardinality partition keys
Enable time-based queries	Encode timestamps in RowKey
Minimize conflicts	Avoid hot partitions (e.g., same user)

RowKey and PartitionKey together form a composite primary key.

Example:

```
{
  "PartitionKey": "tenant-29383",
  "RowKey": "2023-04-01T15:30:00Z"
}
```

Azure Event Hubs

Event Hubs supports partitioned messaging using **partition keys**. All events with the same key land in the same partition, preserving order.

Use case: Order processing, where all events for `order1234` must be processed sequentially.

Send to a partitioned hub in .NET:

```
await eventHubProducer.SendAsync(
  new EventData(Encoding.UTF8.GetBytes(payload)),
```

```
new SendOptions { PartitionKey = "order1234" });
```

Partition design affects consumer scaling and throughput.

Routing and Service Layers

In a sharded system, routing becomes critical. Clients or middle layers must route requests to the correct shard or partition based on the sharding key.

Options:

- **Client-side routing**: SDKs or libraries contain routing logic.

- **Middleware routing**: Services intercept and reroute based on keys.

- **Gateway routing**: API layer abstracts sharding entirely.

For example, in a SaaS platform with `tenantId` as the shard key, requests to `GET /orders` must be rerouted to the correct database:

```
const shard = getShardForTenant(tenantId);
const connection = getSqlConnection(shard);
const result = await connection.query("SELECT * FROM Orders WHERE
TenantId = @tenantId");
```

Avoid over-centralizing routing logic, as it becomes a bottleneck. Design for flexibility and dynamic mapping.

Operational Considerations

Rebalancing Shards

As tenants grow or access patterns change, shards may become unbalanced. Implement migration strategies:

- Move data during low traffic windows

- Use shadow writes to sync during migration

- Use versioned API to gradually switch over

Monitoring

Track partition and shard health:

- Throughput usage per partition (Cosmos DB)

- Storage size and IOPS per disk or DB

- Hot partition detection via metrics (e.g., high RU consumption in one partition)

Use Azure Monitor and custom telemetry to trace query distribution and identify skew.

Backup and DR

Each shard or partition must be backed up independently. Ensure consistent snapshot or backup strategies across shards to support recoverability.

Example:

- Cosmos DB: Continuous backup

- SQL: Geo-redundant automated backups

- PostgreSQL Flexible Server: PITR (Point-in-Time Restore)

Anti-Patterns to Avoid

- **Random partition keys**: Impairs queryability.

- **Low-cardinality keys**: Causes skew and hot partitions.

- **Application-level sharding without abstraction**: Leads to tight coupling.

- **Hard-coded shard logic**: Inflexible and unmaintainable.

Instead, abstract routing logic and centralize metadata about shards in a **shard map** or **routing registry**.

Conclusion

Partitioning and sharding are essential techniques for enabling data platforms to scale horizontally. Whether you're building with Azure Blob Storage, Cosmos DB, Azure SQL, or distributed messaging systems, proper design of partition keys and sharding logic ensures your application performs predictably as data and user volume grow.

Architects must balance performance, manageability, fault isolation, and cost when designing for distribution. A well-sharded system not only scales but also supports operational agility, regional expansion, and multitenancy with confidence.

In the next section, we'll explore storage tiering and lifecycle strategies to manage data aging, retention, and cost optimization in long-running Azure solutions.

Tiered Storage and Lifecycle Management

In cloud-native architectures, data is generated at an unprecedented scale and velocity. From application logs and media assets to transactional records and archival datasets, not all data has the same value over time. A robust storage architecture must therefore implement **tiered storage and lifecycle management** to optimize both performance and cost while ensuring availability and compliance.

Azure offers a rich set of features for classifying, transitioning, and expiring data across storage tiers. This section explores these capabilities in-depth, providing architectural strategies, configuration techniques, and operational best practices for tiered storage and automated data lifecycle policies.

The Need for Tiered Storage

Data usage follows a lifecycle. It begins with frequent access, transitions to infrequent access, and ultimately becomes cold archival or is deleted altogether. Storing all data in a high-performance tier is expensive and unnecessary. Tiered storage enables you to:

1. **Optimize cost** by matching storage tier to data value and access frequency.

2. **Improve performance** by reducing load on high-performance systems.

3. **Ensure compliance** by enforcing retention policies and secure deletion.

4. **Automate governance** by reducing manual overhead with lifecycle rules.

Storage Tiers in Azure

Azure Storage accounts, especially those using **Blob Storage**, support multiple tiers to accommodate various access patterns:

Tier	Description	Typical Use Cases
Hot	High performance, high cost. Frequent access.	Web content, active logs, transactional data
Cool	Lower cost, slightly higher latency. Infrequent use.	Backups, media assets, analytics datasets

Archive Lowest cost, offline access with hours to Compliance archives, historic logs
retrieve.

These tiers can be applied at the **blob level**, and blobs can be **programmatically moved** between tiers or via **automated lifecycle policies**.

Example Tiering Strategy

For a media company:

- **Hot Tier**: Latest uploaded videos for active editing and viewing.

- **Cool Tier**: Published videos with moderate viewership.

- **Archive Tier**: Obsolete or infrequently accessed videos.

For a SaaS platform:

- **Hot Tier**: Last 30 days of logs and audit trails.

- **Cool Tier**: User activity data for analytics >30 days old.

- **Archive Tier**: Regulatory backups older than 1 year.

Implementing Tiered Storage

Blobs can be assigned a tier manually or programmatically using SDKs, REST APIs, or Azure CLI.

CLI Example

```
az storage blob set-tier \
  --account-name mystorageaccount \
  --container-name mycontainer \
  --name file-archive.log \
  --tier Archive
```

SDK Example (Python)

```
from azure.storage.blob import BlobClient

blob = BlobClient.from_connection_string(conn_str, container, blob_name)
blob.set_standard_blob_tier("Cool")
```

Lifecycle Management

To automate movement across tiers and eventual deletion, Azure provides **lifecycle management policies**.

Example JSON policy to move logs to Archive after 90 days and delete after 365 days:

```json
{
  "rules": [
    {
      "enabled": true,
      "name": "log-retention-policy",
      "type": "Lifecycle",
      "definition": {
        "filters": {
          "blobTypes": ["blockBlob"],
          "prefixMatch": ["logs/"]
        },
        "actions": {
          "baseBlob": {
            "tierToCool": {
              "daysAfterModificationGreaterThan": 30
            },
            "tierToArchive": {
              "daysAfterModificationGreaterThan": 90
            },
            "delete": {
              "daysAfterModificationGreaterThan": 365
            }
          }
        }
      }
    }
  ]
}
```

This is configured via the **Azure Portal**, **ARM templates**, **Bicep**, or programmatically via SDKs.

Monitoring and Reporting

To effectively manage tiered storage, visibility is essential.

Azure Monitor Metrics

- **Capacity per tier**: See how much data resides in Hot, Cool, and Archive.

- **Blob count and access metrics**: Understand usage trends.

- **Egress and transaction cost**: Evaluate performance vs. cost trade-offs.

Sample KQL for accessing blob usage trends:

```
StorageBlobLogs
| where OperationName == "GetBlob"
| summarize count() by bin(TimeGenerated, 1d), RequesterIPAddress,
BlobType
```

Use this data to refine lifecycle rules based on actual access patterns.

Cost Optimization Considerations

Storage Cost Per GB

Tier	Approximate Cost per GB (region dependent)
Hot	$0.018–0.024
Cool	$0.01–0.015
Archive	$0.00099–0.003

Additional Costs

- **Read/write transactions**: Cost varies by tier.

- **Data retrieval**: Archive tier incurs charges for rehydration and egress.

- **Early deletion penalties**: Cool (30 days) and Archive (180 days) tiers have minimum retention durations.

Best Practices

- Don't move data to Archive unless you're sure it won't be accessed soon.

- Use Cool tier for medium-term retention where latency tolerance is acceptable.

- Analyze access logs before applying lifecycle policies at scale.

Retention and Compliance

For industries like healthcare, finance, and public sector, retention and deletion policies are critical for compliance with regulations such as:

- **GDPR**: Right to be forgotten.

- **HIPAA**: Secure patient data retention and disposal.

- **SOX**: Retention of financial data.

Azure supports:

- **Immutable blob storage**: Write-once, read-many (WORM) for compliance archives.

- **Legal holds and time-based retention**: Prevent deletion of critical records.

Immutable Blob Policy Example (ARM)

```
{
  "properties": {
    "immutabilityPolicy": {
      "immutabilityPeriodSinceCreationInDays": 365,
      "state": "Locked"
    },
    "hasLegalHold": true
  }
}
```

This prevents tampering and ensures data cannot be deleted for the specified period.

Integration with Azure Data Services

Tiered storage is not isolated. It integrates across the Azure ecosystem:

- **Azure Synapse**: Read cool-tier blobs for analytics workloads.

- **Azure Data Factory**: Move data between storage tiers or accounts.

- **Azure Logic Apps / Functions**: Trigger tier transitions or audits.

- **Azure Purview**: Discover and classify data across storage tiers.

You can design event-driven automation—for instance, move data to Archive when metadata flags it as "expired" or when no read operations have occurred for 90+ days.

Real-World Pattern: Data Lake with Lifecycle Tiers

In a modern data lake architecture:

- **Raw zone (Hot)**: Data freshly ingested.

- **Processed zone (Cool)**: Cleaned and transformed datasets.

- **Archive zone (Archive)**: Long-term storage of historic data.

Azure Data Lake Storage Gen2 supports this model with **hierarchical namespaces**, enabling folder-based lifecycle policies:

```
"prefixMatch": ["raw/logs/", "processed/year=2021/"]
```

Tiering strategies can be based on ingestion time, data classification, or business rules.

Programmatic Lifecycle Governance

Use Azure SDKs and tools like Terraform, Bicep, or ARM to define tiering policies as code. This ensures:

- Consistent application across environments

- Auditable changes and version control

- Easy rollback and policy update automation

Example Bicep definition:

```
resource                                              lifecycle
'Microsoft.Storage/storageAccounts/managementPolicies@2021-04-01'   =
{
  name: '${storageAccount.name}/default'
  properties: {
    policy: {
      rules: [
```

```
{
  name: 'archiveRule'
  enabled: true
  definition: {
    filters: {
      blobTypes: ['blockBlob']
      prefixMatch: ['archive/']
    }
    actions: {
      baseBlob: {
        tierToCool: {
          daysAfterModificationGreaterThan: 30
        }
        tierToArchive: {
          daysAfterModificationGreaterThan: 90
        }
      }
    }
  }
}
]
}
}
}
```

This codifies your storage lifecycle and aligns with Infrastructure-as-Code (IaC) practices.

Challenges and Mitigations

Challenge	Mitigation
Unexpected access to archived data	Add delay buffer before archive; monitor access logs
Policy misconfiguration	Test in non-production; review in Azure Policy or Management Portal
Complex data categorization	Use metadata tags, naming conventions, and classification tools

| Cross-region needs | compliance | Use geo-redundant storage with region-based tiering policies |

Conclusion

Tiered storage and lifecycle management are not optional in a scalable cloud architecture—they are essential. By intelligently assigning storage tiers and automating transitions based on data age, access frequency, and business logic, architects can drastically reduce costs, improve system performance, and simplify compliance.

Azure provides the tooling and flexibility to implement these strategies at any scale—from small teams managing app logs to global enterprises with petabytes of archival data. In the next chapter, we'll shift focus from storage to databases, beginning with scalable relational designs in Azure SQL and the Hyperscale architecture.

Chapter 5: Building Scalable Databases in Azure

SQL Database Elastic Pools and Hyperscale

Relational databases continue to power a significant portion of enterprise applications. As workloads grow in complexity and volume, database scalability becomes critical to maintaining performance, cost efficiency, and availability. Azure provides powerful options to meet these challenges—most notably **Azure SQL Database Elastic Pools** and **Azure SQL Hyperscale**.

This section explores these technologies in detail, focusing on their architecture, use cases, performance characteristics, deployment strategies, and operational best practices. Architects will learn how to choose between them and integrate them effectively into scalable cloud-native solutions.

Azure SQL Database Models: An Overview

Azure SQL Database is a fully managed Platform-as-a-Service (PaaS) offering that abstracts away infrastructure concerns like OS patching, backups, high availability, and upgrades.

There are three primary deployment models:

1. **Single Database** – Isolated and independently managed instance.

2. **Elastic Pool** – Group of databases that share a pool of resources.

3. **Managed Instance** – Near full compatibility with SQL Server, suitable for lift-and-shift.

Elastic Pools and Hyperscale are two strategies specifically designed to support scale in different dimensions—**multi-database workloads** and **high-volume transactional systems**, respectively.

Elastic Pools: Shared Resources, Dynamic Scale

An **Elastic Pool** is a shared compute and storage pool that hosts multiple Azure SQL databases. It is ideal for scenarios where multiple databases have **unpredictable or cyclical usage patterns**, enabling them to dynamically share resources.

Key Characteristics

- **Shared** **DTUs/vCores** across databases

- **Per-database** resource limits
- **Automatic** scaling within the pool
- **Built-in** high availability
- Cost savings over provisioning single databases

Common Use Cases

- Multi-tenant SaaS platforms where each customer has a separate database
- Applications with bursty or inconsistent database workloads
- Departmental apps with lightweight, varying usage patterns
- Development and testing environments

Architecture Example

Imagine a pool with 10 customer databases. Instead of provisioning each one with 50 DTUs individually (total 500 DTUs), you can assign a pool of 300 DTUs that all databases draw from as needed.

This reduces cost and resource waste.

Provisioning an Elastic Pool (Bicep)

```
resource sqlPool 'Microsoft.Sql/servers/elasticPools@2022-02-01-
preview' = {
  name: 'customerPool'
  parent: sqlServer
  location: resourceGroup().location
  sku: {
    name: 'StandardPool'
    tier: 'Standard'
    capacity: 100
  }
  properties: {
    maxSizeBytes: 536870912000
    perDatabaseSettings: {
      minCapacity: 5
      maxCapacity: 50
    }
  }
}
```

```
}
```

Databases added to this pool will respect the min/max per-database capacity while drawing from the shared pool.

Performance Tuning Tips

- Use **Query Store** to track query performance across tenants.

- Enable **automatic tuning** to fix regressions.

- Monitor resource utilization using **Azure Monitor** and **Intelligent Insights**.

- Implement **connection pooling** in your application code to avoid exhausting pool connections.

Azure SQL Hyperscale: Scaling Beyond Limits

For high-throughput, data-intensive applications, Azure SQL Hyperscale offers a radically different architecture from traditional Azure SQL Database.

What is Hyperscale?

Hyperscale is a **cloud-native architecture** that separates compute, log, and storage layers to enable near-infinite scaling.

Layer	Function
Compute	Runs query engine and session logic
Log Service	Accepts and replicates transactions
Page Server	Maintains data files in memory-mapped pages
Storage	Durable storage backed by Azure Blob Storage

This decoupling allows scaling each component independently.

Key Capabilities

- Up to **100 TB** of database size

- Near-instant scaling of compute nodes (up/down)
- **Fast backups** and restores regardless of size
- Read scale-out with **read replicas**
- Rapid data ingestion and recovery

Use Cases

- Large transactional systems (e-commerce, ERP)
- Real-time analytics and reporting workloads
- Data warehousing without moving to Synapse
- Geo-distributed, high-throughput SaaS platforms

Hyperscale Advantages

- Faster **provisioning and failover**
- No downtime during backups
- Long-running queries handled efficiently
- Separation of write and read workloads

Creating a Hyperscale Database (ARM/Bicep)

```
resource hyperscaleDb 'Microsoft.Sql/servers/databases@2022-02-01-
preview' = {
  name: 'transactions-db'
  parent: sqlServer
  location: resourceGroup().location
  sku: {
    name: 'HS_Gen5_4'
    tier: 'Hyperscale'
    capacity: 4
  }
  properties: {
    maxSizeBytes: 109951162777600
    zoneRedundant: true
  }
```

```
}
```

You can also scale read replicas independently and direct reporting workloads to them.

Comparing Elastic Pools vs. Hyperscale

Feature	Elastic Pool	Hyperscale
Target Scenario	Many small/medium workloads	Large-scale transactional workloads
Architecture	Shared pool, single engine	Decoupled compute/log/storage
Max Database Size	4 TB	100 TB+
Performance Focus	Cost optimization	Throughput and scalability
Read Scale-out	Not supported	Supported with multiple read replicas
Best for SaaS?	Yes, multi-tenant app DBs	Yes, for high-volume tenants
Cost Efficiency	High for many small DBs	High for large data volumes

---

Integrating Elastic Pools with SaaS Architecture

Elastic Pools are particularly well-suited to **multi-tenant SaaS** models where each tenant has an isolated database, but workloads vary.

Example Pattern

- Use `tenantId` to route to the correct database
- Provision a **per-tenant** **schema** or full DB
- Monitor usage and autoscale or migrate high-volume tenants to dedicated Hyperscale DBs

```
public SqlConnection GetTenantConnection(string tenantId)
{
```

```
    string connString = tenantMap[tenantId];
    return new SqlConnection(connString);
}
```

With Azure Elastic Jobs or Logic Apps, you can automate tasks like schema updates, performance tuning, and backups across all tenant databases in the pool.

Monitoring and Maintenance

Both Elastic Pools and Hyperscale integrate with:

- **Azure Monitor**: Query performance, DTU/vCore usage
- **Log Analytics**: Centralized diagnostics and telemetry
- **SQL Insights**: Deep visibility into database health
- **Automatic tuning**: Index creation, plan correction

Use **Intelligent Insights** to receive recommendations based on observed workload patterns.

Kusto query to monitor DTU utilization across databases:

```
AzureDiagnostics
| where ResourceType == "DATABASE"
| summarize avg(avg_dtu_percent_s) by Resource, bin(TimeGenerated,
5m)
```

For Hyperscale, monitor page server and compute metrics independently to tune performance.

Best Practices

- **Elastic Pools**:
  - Keep usage variance high between databases to maximize cost savings.
  - Avoid pooling databases with consistently high usage.
  - Use naming conventions and tagging to manage tenant DBs.

- **Hyperscale**:

    - Use read replicas to offload reporting workloads.

    - Design for concurrent ingest and analytics.

    - Take advantage of fast restores for dev/test environments.

- **General**:

    - Use **Private Endpoints** for secure access.

    - Encrypt with **customer-managed keys** if regulatory requirements demand.

    - Enable **Advanced Threat Protection** for real-time security alerts.

Conclusion

Azure SQL Database Elastic Pools and Hyperscale represent two powerful but distinct strategies for scaling relational data in the cloud. Elastic Pools provide cost-effective scaling for many small, unpredictable workloads—ideal for SaaS and departmental apps. Hyperscale, on the other hand, unleashes extreme scalability for high-throughput, large-volume systems, with advanced architectural features not available in traditional SQL deployments.

Architects must evaluate application patterns, workload profiles, growth projections, and performance demands to select the right model—or, in hybrid environments, combine both to deliver optimal results.

In the next section, we'll explore Cosmos DB, Azure's globally distributed NoSQL database, and how to design its partitions, consistency models, and global replication strategy for truly planetary scale.

Cosmos DB Global Distribution and Partitioning

Azure Cosmos DB is Microsoft's globally distributed, multi-model NoSQL database built for mission-critical applications that require guaranteed low-latency, high-throughput, and elastic scalability. Designed from the ground up for horizontal scale, Cosmos DB offers architects a platform that abstracts the complexities of distributed databases while providing robust SLAs for availability, latency, consistency, and throughput.

One of Cosmos DB's core strengths is its ability to **distribute data across multiple Azure regions** with automatic replication and failover. Combined with its **partitioning model**, Cosmos DB supports applications with billions of data items and petabyte-scale storage—while still delivering millisecond latency.

In this section, we will cover:

- How Cosmos DB achieves global distribution
- Partitioning strategies and best practices
- Data modeling for distributed workloads
- Multi-region writes and failover patterns
- Designing for consistency, availability, and performance
- Real-world use cases and implementation techniques

Global Distribution in Cosmos DB

Cosmos DB allows databases and containers to be **replicated automatically across any number of Azure regions**. With just a few clicks or lines of code, data becomes globally available, with the platform handling the complexities of synchronization, routing, and failover.

Key Capabilities

- **Multi-region read and write support**
- **Automatic failover with region priorities**
- **Multi-master (active-active) configuration**
- **Data replicated via asynchronous, near-real-time propagation**
- SLA-backed **99.999% availability** when distributed across multiple regions

Configuring Global Distribution

Global replication can be configured through the Azure Portal, ARM, Bicep, CLI, or SDKs.

Bicep example:

```
resource cosmosAccount 'Microsoft.DocumentDB/databaseAccounts@2021-
10-15' = {
  name: 'mycosmosdb'
  location: 'East US'
  kind: 'GlobalDocumentDB'
  properties: {
```

```
    databaseAccountOfferType: 'Standard'
    locations: [
      {
        locationName: 'East US'
        failoverPriority: 0
        isZoneRedundant: false
      }
      {
        locationName: 'West Europe'
        failoverPriority: 1
        isZoneRedundant: true
      }
    ]
    enableMultipleWriteLocations: true
    consistencyPolicy: {
      defaultConsistencyLevel: 'Session'
    }
  }
}
```

Partitioning in Cosmos DB

Every Cosmos DB container must have a **partition key**, which is used to distribute data across physical partitions (shards). Each logical partition contains items that share the same partition key value.

Why Partitioning Matters

1. **Performance**: Enables horizontal scale by spreading requests across partitions.

2. **Throughput**: Avoids bottlenecks and hot partitions by distributing RU/s.

3. **Storage**: Logical partitions are limited to 20GB; proper partitioning is essential.

4. **Consistency**: Partition keys influence transaction scope and latency.

Choosing a Partition Key

The partition key should be selected based on the application's access pattern, write throughput, and storage needs. A good partition key ensures **even distribution** of data and **predictable access**.

Partition Key	Pros	Cons
/userId	Distributes per user, good for multi-tenant	Hotspot if one user is very active
/orderId	Very granular, good for item-level access	Poor for querying across orders
/region	Aligns to geo-querying	Hot partitions if one region dominates traffic
/deviceId	Useful for IoT workloads	May need to aggregate across many devices

Ideal characteristics:

- High   cardinality

- Even   read/write   distribution

- Aligned   with   query   and   transaction   boundaries

Modeling Data for Distribution

Cosmos DB is **schema-agnostic**, meaning documents within a container can have different structures. Data modeling should consider:

- **Denormalization**:   Embed   frequently   accessed   related   data

- **Reference   patterns**:   Link   related   entities   via   ID

- **Time-series modeling**: Use composite keys like /deviceId/timestamp for IoT data

Example document:

{

```
  "id": "order-123",
  "partitionKey": "user-456",
  "userId": "user-456",
  "orderDate": "2025-04-01T12:00:00Z",
  "items": [
    { "sku": "abc", "qty": 1 },
    { "sku": "def", "qty": 2 }
  ],
  "status": "Processing"
}
```

Throughput and Request Units (RU/s)

Cosmos DB charges throughput in **Request Units (RU/s)**, which represent the cost of operations. Each container must be provisioned with RU/s capacity—either fixed or auto-scaled.

Throughput Modes

- **Provisioned throughput**: Pre-allocated RU/s per container or shared at database level.

- **Autoscale**: Automatically scales RU/s based on demand (max 10x min RU).

- **Serverless**: Pay-per-request for small, sporadic workloads.

RU costs vary:

- Read 1KB document: ~1 RU

- Write 1KB document: ~5 RU

- Query with filters: Varies by complexity and indexing

Use **Azure Metrics Explorer** or **Query Metrics** to monitor and tune usage.

Consistency Models

Cosmos DB supports five consistency levels, giving architects control over the trade-off between consistency and performance.

Level	Guarantees	Latency	Availability
Strong	Linearizability	High	Region-tied
Bounded staleness	Configurable lag window	Medium	Regional
Session	Consistent within client session	Low	Global
Consistent prefix	Order preserved, gaps allowed	Low	Global
Eventual	No ordering, eventual convergence	Lowest	Highest

Session consistency is the default and recommended for most applications. It ensures reads reflect writes from the same session without the latency overhead of strong consistency.

Multi-region Writes and Conflict Resolution

When **multi-master** writes are enabled, Cosmos DB allows concurrent writes to any region.

Use cases:

- Global apps with write-local latency requirements
- Real-time collaboration platforms
- Offline-first mobile apps syncing from multiple regions

Cosmos DB handles replication and supports multiple **conflict resolution policies**:

- **Last writer wins (LWW)**: Based on a field like timestamp or version.
- **Custom logic**: Use stored procedures to define resolution rules.

Example enabling LWW:

```
"conflictResolutionPolicy": {
  "mode": "LastWriterWins",
  "conflictResolutionPath": "/modifiedAt"
}
```

Conflicts can be logged and inspected for auditing or manual correction.

High Availability and Disaster Recovery

Cosmos DB offers 99.999% availability with multi-region write/read and **automatic failover**. Architects can configure **region failover priority**, and Cosmos DB ensures RTO < 5 seconds.

Enable **multi-region write** for zero-downtime deployments and resilience:

- Read/write in any region

- Auto-failover during outages

- Geo-replicated backups and point-in-time restore

Use **private endpoints** and **firewall rules** to secure access across regions.

Monitoring and Optimization

Use the following tools to monitor and optimize Cosmos DB:

- **Azure Monitor**: Track RU consumption, latency, availability.

- **Query Metrics**: View RU cost per query.

- **Index Advisor**: Auto-suggests index improvements.

- **Diagnostics Logs**: Capture errors, throttling, connection issues.

KQL Example – Top 5 throttled operations:

```
CosmosDbOperation
| where StatusCode == 429
| summarize Count = count() by ResourceId, OperationName
| top 5 by Count
```

Use this insight to refactor access patterns or increase RU/s allocation.

Security and Compliance

Cosmos DB supports:

- **Role-based** **access** **control** **(RBAC)**
- **Managed** **identities** **for** **access**
- **Encryption** **at** **rest** **and** **in** **transit**
- **Customer-managed** **keys** **(CMK)**
- **Private** **Link** for secure VNet access
- **Audit** **logs** for regulatory compliance

Use **Azure Policy** to enforce required configurations across environments.

Real-world Use Cases

- **Retail**: Product catalog with global consistency and regional updates.
- **Gaming**: Leaderboards and player stats across continents.
- **IoT**: Device telemetry ingestion with time-series modeling.
- **Finance**: Fraud detection across geographies with low-latency writes.
- **Healthcare**: Patient data storage with consistency guarantees and audit trails.

Each scenario benefits from Cosmos DB's global footprint, partitioning, and throughput capabilities.

Conclusion

Cosmos DB is a powerful enabler for globally distributed, high-scale applications. By understanding and leveraging its partitioning model and global distribution capabilities, architects can build data layers that are resilient, performant, and aligned with modern user expectations.

From selecting an effective partition key to choosing the right consistency model and configuring multi-region writes, every decision impacts performance, cost, and user experience. With thoughtful design and continuous monitoring, Cosmos DB becomes the foundation for cloud applications that operate at planetary scale.

In the next section, we'll look at caching and read replica strategies to further boost performance and reduce costs for high-throughput systems in Azure.

Caching Strategies and Read Replicas

In modern cloud architectures, where performance, scalability, and user experience are critical, **caching** and **read replicas** serve as essential techniques to offload primary databases, reduce latency, and increase application responsiveness. While Azure provides robust database engines like SQL Database and Cosmos DB, relying solely on them for every data access can lead to bottlenecks, excessive costs, or degraded performance under high load.

This section explores how caching and read replicas can be effectively applied across Azure services. We'll cover types of caching, architectural patterns, Azure-native services like Azure Cache for Redis, SQL read replicas, Cosmos DB dedicated replicas, and hybrid approaches that blend multiple strategies for optimal results.

Why Use Caching and Read Replicas?

Caching and read replicas serve overlapping but distinct goals:

- **Caching**: Temporarily stores frequently accessed or computed data in memory to reduce load and latency.

- **Read Replicas**: Provide additional read-only copies of a database for scaling read workloads.

Benefits

Benefit	Caching	Read Replicas
Low-latency access	✓ Millisecond response time	✓ Read-local replicas
Reduce primary DB load	✓ Offload hot data reads	✓ Offload complex read queries
High availability	⚠ Depends on cache configuration	✓ Redundant copies across regions
Cost efficiency	✓ Reduces RU/s or DTU usage	⚠ Adds extra DB cost

| Stale data risk | ✓ Yes (must manage expiry) | ⚠ Eventual consistency possible |

Use caching for ephemeral, frequently accessed data and read replicas for consistent, operationally sound scale-out of read operations.

Caching Techniques

1. In-Memory Caching

Azure Cache for Redis is the primary service used for in-memory caching in Azure. It provides a high-performance, low-latency data store that supports key-value, sorted sets, pub/sub, and TTL.

Common use cases:

- Caching session state or user profiles

- Temporary storage of API responses

- Rate limiting and token validation

- Leaderboards and ranking systems

Example: Caching product data in Node.js

```
const redis = require("redis");
const client = redis.createClient();

async function getProduct(productId) {
  const cached = await client.getAsync(productId);
  if (cached) return JSON.parse(cached);

  const product = await db.getProduct(productId); // expensive call
  await client.setex(productId, 300, JSON.stringify(product));
  return product;
}
```

Redis supports TTLs, eviction policies, and clustering for scale.

Eviction Policies

Redis allows configuration of eviction policies to handle memory limits:

- **LRU** (Least Recently Used)

- **LFU** (Least Frequently Used)

- **Volatile TTL** – evict keys with TTL only

Ensure appropriate expiry settings (EX, PX, TTL) to avoid stale data issues.

---

2. Application-Level Caching

Client-side caching in web or mobile applications can dramatically reduce redundant server requests.

Strategies include:

- HTTP caching with ETag, Cache-Control, and Last-Modified headers

- Service workers in PWAs to cache assets and data

- CDN integration (e.g., Azure CDN) for caching static content

Example cache-control headers in Azure App Service:

```
"headers": [
  {
    "name": "Cache-Control",
    "value": "public, max-age=3600"
  }
]
```

This approach reduces round trips and speeds up rendering.

---

3. Distributed Caching in Microservices

In distributed systems, a centralized Redis cache can be shared across services for:

- Authorization token validation

- Caching configuration settings

- Cross-service communication (via pub/sub)

Key pattern: **cache-aside**

- Read from cache
- If miss, read from DB and populate cache

Other patterns include:

- **Write-through**: Write to cache and database simultaneously
- **Write-behind**: Queue writes to DB asynchronously
- **Read-through**: Cache abstracts the database read

Read Replicas in Azure SQL

Azure SQL Database supports **active geo-replication** and **auto-failover groups** to create read replicas in the same or different regions.

Active Geo-Replication

- Up to 4 readable secondaries
- Manual read routing
- Asynchronous replication (eventual consistency)
- Read-only endpoint

Auto-Failover Groups

- Automatic failover to secondary region
- Shared listener for applications
- Read endpoint for reporting workloads

Use case: Reporting portal reads from the secondary replica while writes go to the primary.

Example Bicep setup:

```
resource failoverGroup 'Microsoft.Sql/servers/failoverGroups@2021-02-01-preview' = {
```

```
  name: 'global-fog'
  parent: sqlPrimary
  properties: {
    partnerServers: [
      {
        id: resourceId('Microsoft.Sql/servers', 'sql-secondary')
      }
    ]
    readWriteEndpoint: {
      failoverPolicy: 'Automatic'
      failoverWithDataLossGracePeriodMinutes: 60
    }
    readOnlyEndpoint: {
      failoverPolicy: 'Disabled'
    }
  }
}
```

Cosmos DB Read Replicas

With **multi-region read replicas**, Cosmos DB automatically routes read operations to the nearest region to minimize latency.

- Built-in when multiple regions are configured

- Clients connect via SDK and Cosmos decides routing

- Read preference settings (e.g., preferred region list)

Use **read regions** to serve content closer to users and distribute analytical workloads.

Query across regions using SDK configuration:

```
CosmosClientOptions options = new CosmosClientOptions
{
  ApplicationPreferredRegions = new List<string> { "West Europe",
"East US" }
};
```

This ensures low-latency access with high availability.

Caching Patterns with Databases

1. **Metadata**   **Caching**

Store table schema, config flags, and authorization rules in Redis to avoid frequent DB reads.

2. **Materialized**   **Views**

For complex joins or aggregations, cache results in Redis or a separate reporting DB.

3. **Query**   **Result**   **Caching**

Cache popular or expensive queries, especially in BI/reporting dashboards.

4. **Time-Series**   **Caching**

For IoT and telemetry, cache most recent readings to support real-time graphs.

5. **Write**   **Buffering**

Use Redis to collect bursts of writes, then flush to the database asynchronously for ingestion scenarios.

Monitoring and Expiry Management

- Use **Azure Monitor** with Redis integration to track memory usage, hit/miss ratio, and evictions.

- Configure **alerts** for high CPU, memory pressure, or slow queries.

- Enable **cache busting** on updates—either via TTL expiration or cache key versioning.

Example: Cache key versioning

```
const key = `user-profile:${userId}:v2`; // v2 triggers reload
```

Security and Compliance

Redis on Azure supports:

- **Private** **endpoints**
- **TLS** **encryption** **in** **transit**
- **VNet** **injection** **(Premium** **tier)**
- **Managed** **identities** **for** **auth**
- **IP** **firewall** **rules**

For read replicas:

- Use **RBAC** **and** **firewall** to control access
- Monitor **replication** **lag** for data freshness
- Audit logs for reads from replica regions

Combining Caching and Replication

Advanced scenarios often combine caching and read replicas:

- Use **Redis** **for** **hot** **data,** **replica** **for** **cold** **data**
- Cache frequently accessed query results from replicas
- Load balance between **primary read** and **replica read** based on latency or cost

Example architecture:

- Web App → Redis (read/write cache)
- If miss → SQL read replica
- Writes → SQL primary
- Background job syncs complex computed results to Redis

Best Practices

Practice	Why It Matters
Choose appropriate TTL	Prevents stale data while avoiding cache churn
Use cache keys with clear structure	Easier invalidation and debugging
Secure Redis with Private Link	Prevents exposure to public internet
Avoid storing large blobs in cache	Use blob storage and cache metadata instead
Use autoscale or clusters for Redis	Handles dynamic workload and improves availability
Design for failover of replicas	Applications should retry or reroute on failures

Conclusion

Caching and read replicas are essential tools for architects building performant and scalable applications on Azure. Whether it's reducing latency for real-time applications, scaling read-heavy workloads, or improving cost efficiency, these techniques unlock significant gains across diverse scenarios.

By leveraging Azure Cache for Redis, SQL Database replicas, and Cosmos DB regional reads, architects can construct intelligent data access layers that deliver seamless experiences to users worldwide. When combined with observability, TTL governance, and secure connectivity, caching and replication become more than optimization tactics—they become pillars of resilient cloud-native systems.

In the next chapter, we will shift from databases to networking, exploring scalable patterns using Azure Load Balancer, Application Gateway, and hybrid network strategies for global applications.

Chapter 6: Designing for Scalable Networking

Azure Load Balancer and Application Gateway

As applications scale and evolve into distributed systems, **network traffic management** becomes a critical concern for availability, resilience, performance, and security. Azure provides a rich set of load balancing services—each optimized for different layers of the networking stack. Among these, **Azure Load Balancer** and **Azure Application Gateway** are foundational components for achieving scalable, fault-tolerant architectures.

This section provides a deep dive into how these services work, when and how to use them, their configurations, architectural patterns, and real-world integration strategies. You'll also learn to design for redundancy, health monitoring, and secure traffic flow.

Load Balancing in Azure: Conceptual Overview

In Azure, load balancing happens across multiple layers:

Layer	Service	Protocols	Description
Network (L4)	Azure Load Balancer	TCP/UDP	Distributes traffic across VMs/VMSS
Application (L7)	Azure Application Gateway	HTTP/HTTPS	Routes traffic based on URL, headers, etc.
Global (DNS)	Azure Traffic Manager	DNS	Routes traffic based on geographic proximity
Global (Anycast)	Azure Front Door	HTTP/HTTPS	Provides global HTTP routing, WAF, caching

This section focuses on **Load Balancer** and **Application Gateway**, which operate within regions and are used to distribute traffic across backend pools within or across availability zones.

Azure Load Balancer

Azure Load Balancer is a high-performance, ultra-low-latency Layer 4 (TCP/UDP) load balancer. It is ideal for balancing traffic between virtual machines, scale sets, and services inside a virtual network.

Key Features

- Layer 4 (Transport layer) load balancing
- Inbound and outbound scenarios
- High throughput and low latency
- Zone redundant and availability zone aware
- NAT rules for port forwarding
- Health probes for availability checks

Load Balancer Types

Type	Use Case
Public	Exposes services to the internet
Internal	Balances traffic within a VNet (east-west)

Use Cases

- High-throughput, low-latency backend services
- SQL Server Always On Availability Groups
- VPN gateway load balancing
- Game server deployments
- NAT scenarios for VM port mapping

Configuration Example

Bicep example to configure a Public Load Balancer:

```
resource publicIP 'Microsoft.Network/publicIPAddresses@2022-01-01' =
{
  name: 'app-lb-ip'
```

```
    location: resourceGroup().location
    sku: {
      name: 'Standard'
    }
    properties: {
      publicIPAllocationMethod: 'Static'
    }
}

resource loadBalancer 'Microsoft.Network/loadBalancers@2022-01-01' =
{
  name: 'app-loadbalancer'
  location: resourceGroup().location
  sku: {
    name: 'Standard'
  }
  properties: {
    frontendIPConfigurations: [
      {
        name: 'LoadBalancerFrontEnd'
        properties: {
          publicIPAddress: {
            id: publicIP.id
          }
        }
      }
    ]
    backendAddressPools: [
      {
        name: 'BackendPool'
      }
    ]
    loadBalancingRules: [
      {
        name: 'http-rule'
        properties: {
          protocol: 'Tcp'
          frontendPort: 80
          backendPort: 80
          frontendIPConfiguration: {
```

```
          id:
'${loadBalancer.id}/frontendIPConfigurations/LoadBalancerFrontEnd'
        }
        backendAddressPool: {
          id: '${loadBalancer.id}/backendAddressPools/BackendPool'
        }
        probe: {
          id: '${loadBalancer.id}/probes/HealthProbe'
        }
      }
    }
  ]
  probes: [
    {
      name: 'HealthProbe'
      properties: {
        protocol: 'Http'
        port: 80
        requestPath: '/health'
        intervalInSeconds: 5
        numberOfProbes: 2
      }
    }
  ]
}
}
```

This configuration balances incoming HTTP traffic to VM instances based on health probe results.

Azure Application Gateway

Azure Application Gateway is a Layer 7 load balancer with advanced routing capabilities. It understands HTTP, HTTPS, and WebSocket protocols, allowing for intelligent request handling.

Key Features

- URL-based   routing   (path-based)

- Host   name-based   routing

- SSL termination and end-to-end SSL
- Web Application Firewall (WAF)
- Rewrite HTTP headers and query strings
- Connection draining and session affinity
- Autoscaling SKU available (v2)

Use Cases

- Modern web applications with routing needs
- Multi-tenant SaaS frontends
- API gateway pattern with routing by service
- Protection against OWASP top 10 threats using WAF
- Blue/green deployments via weighted backend rules

App Gateway vs. Load Balancer

Feature	Azure Load Balancer	Azure Application Gateway
Layer	L4 (TCP/UDP)	L7 (HTTP/HTTPS)
Protocol awareness	No	Yes
URL/path routing	No	Yes
SSL offloading	No	Yes
Web Application Firewall	No	Yes
Best suited for	Infrastructure traffic	Web applications, APIs

---

Routing Configuration with App Gateway

App Gateway uses **listeners**, **rules**, and **backend pools** to manage routing.

Sample rule structure:

- Listener on port 443 with SSL certificate

- Rule: If path starts with `/api`, route to backend A; else route to backend B

- Backend pool: VMSS, AKS ingress, App Service, or static IPs

Example JSON for rule (conceptual):

```json
{
  "ruleName": "route-by-path",
  "priority": 10,
  "ruleType": "PathBasedRouting",
  "paths": ["/api/*"],
  "backendPool": "api-backend"
}
```

Use Azure CLI or Bicep to configure routes, backends, and probe paths.

Application Gateway Integration Patterns

1. **With Azure Kubernetes Service (AKS)**
   - Use **AGIC (Application Gateway Ingress Controller)**
   - Routes external traffic directly to Kubernetes services
   - Combines K8s-native manifests with L7 App Gateway features

2. **With App Services**
   - Use **App Service as backend** with host-based routing
   - Enables centralized entry point for multiple PaaS apps

3. **With Azure Firewall or Front Door**
   - Use in a **hub-spoke model** with Firewall in hub
   - App Gateway in spoke for per-app routing and WAF

4. **With Private Link**

- Route traffic to internal endpoints secured with Private Link
- Use internal App Gateway for fully private access

Monitoring and Diagnostics

Both services integrate with Azure Monitor and Network Watcher.

- **Metrics**: Throughput, health probe status, connection count
- **Logs**: Request tracing, access logs, performance diagnostics
- **Alerts**: Custom thresholds on 5xx responses, latency, or probe failures

Kusto Query Language example:

```
AzureDiagnostics
| where ResourceType == "APPLICATIONGATEWAYS"
| where httpStatus_d >= 500
| summarize count() by requestUri_s, httpStatus_d
```

Use **Log Analytics Workspace** for centralized diagnostics and dashboards.

Security Considerations

- Use **WAF** on Application Gateway to inspect HTTP/S traffic
- Enable **SSL end-to-end encryption**
- Use **Private IP** for internal-only access
- Restrict backend access with **NSGs and ASGs**
- Integrate with **Azure Policy** to enforce configurations

Performance and Availability

- **Standard Load Balancer** supports 1,000+ VMs with ultra-low latency.

- **App Gateway v2 SKU** supports autoscaling and zone redundancy.

- Both services support **multi-zone deployment** for HA.

- Use **custom health probes** to ensure only healthy backends serve traffic.

High-Availability Design Patterns

1. **Zone Redundant Load Balancer** with VMSS across zones

2. **Active-Passive App Gateway** with Traffic Manager for regional failover

3. **Blue-Green Deployment** with App Gateway path-based routing

4. Global Front Door → Regional App Gateway → Internal Load Balancer for end-to-end global-to-local routing

Conclusion

Azure Load Balancer and Application Gateway are core components of scalable networking design. Load Balancer handles high-performance L4 traffic distribution, ideal for infrastructure services, while Application Gateway manages intelligent L7 routing with SSL offload and WAF protection.

Choosing the right service—or combining both strategically—enables architects to deliver fast, secure, and highly available user experiences. With monitoring, autoscaling, and policy enforcement built-in, these services provide the robust networking foundation for resilient cloud applications.

Next, we'll extend this networking foundation with Azure Front Door and Traffic Manager to support global routing, latency optimization, and multi-region architecture at scale.

Azure Front Door and Traffic Manager

In globally distributed applications, ensuring fast, reliable, and secure delivery of content to users across geographies is a foundational requirement. Azure provides two powerful services—**Azure Front Door** and **Azure Traffic Manager**—that enable architects to build globally resilient applications with low latency, high availability, and intelligent routing. Though they serve overlapping purposes, each is optimized for different layers and workloads.

This section examines Azure Front Door and Azure Traffic Manager in depth, comparing their capabilities, use cases, and integration patterns. You'll learn how to use them to implement performance optimization, failover routing, health monitoring, geographic steering, and multi-region deployment strategies that meet global-scale demands.

The Challenge of Global Networking

Traditional web and application architectures often suffer from:

- **High latency** for distant users

- **Single-region failures**

- **Inefficient routing** under failover or disaster conditions

- **DNS-level limitations** that lack protocol awareness

Azure Front Door and Traffic Manager resolve these challenges by enabling **application-layer and DNS-layer routing**, bringing content and logic closer to users, and ensuring resilience during infrastructure or regional disruptions.

Azure Front Door

Azure Front Door is a global, Layer 7 reverse proxy and application delivery network. It uses Microsoft's Anycast-based edge network to direct user traffic to the nearest available backend, while also providing acceleration, TLS offloading, WAF, caching, and advanced routing rules.

Key Features

- Global HTTP/HTTPS routing via Anycast

- Path-based and host-based routing

- Web Application Firewall (WAF)

- URL rewrite and redirect

- SSL termination and custom domains

- Session affinity (cookie-based)

- Fast failover with health probes

- CDN-like content acceleration

When to Use Front Door

- Applications needing **low-latency global access**
- SaaS platforms with **geo-distributed frontends**
- API gateways with **centralized security**
- Single-entry point for **multi-region backends**
- Enhancing security with **WAF and DDoS protection**

Architecture Overview

Front Door sits at the **edge**, processing requests before they enter your Azure region. Traffic is routed via:

1. **Frontend hosts** (your custom domain or subdomain)
2. **Routing rules** (map path/host to backends)
3. **Backend pools** (App Services, VMSS, AKS, or external endpoints)

Example scenario: `api.yourapp.com` routes `/v1/users` to the UK backend and `/v1/payments` to the US backend.

Configuring Azure Front Door (v2)

Azure Front Door Standard and Premium tiers offer advanced security, rule engine, private link integration, and enhanced observability.

Backend Pool Sample (Bicep)

```
resource frontDoor 'Microsoft.Cdn/profiles/afdEndpoints@2021-06-01' =
{
  name: 'global-endpoint'
  parent: cdnProfile
  location: 'Global'
  properties: {
    originGroups: [
      {
```

```
name: 'backendpool'
properties: {
  healthProbeSettings: {
    protocol: 'Https'
    path: '/health'
    intervalInSeconds: 30
    healthProbeMethod: 'GET'
  }
  origins: [
    {
      name: 'uk-backend'
      properties: {
        hostName: 'app-uk.azurewebsites.net'
      }
    },
    {
      name: 'us-backend'
      properties: {
        hostName: 'app-us.azurewebsites.net'
      }
    }
  ]
}
}
]
}
}
```

Routing Rule Example

- If   request   path   =   /images/*,   route   to   origin   group   A

- If   request   path   =   /api/*,   route   to   origin   group   B

- Use rules engine to enforce HTTPS, add headers, and apply caching policies

---

Azure Traffic Manager

Azure Traffic Manager is a DNS-based traffic load balancer that routes user requests to the appropriate endpoint based on policies like performance, priority, or geographic rules. Unlike

Front Door, it operates at **Layer 3/4**, manipulating DNS responses rather than inspecting HTTP requests.

Key Features

- DNS-based routing with custom profiles
- Geographic routing and traffic steering
- Performance-based routing (lowest latency)
- Weighted routing for gradual rollout or testing
- Priority-based failover
- Endpoint health monitoring
- Works across Azure and non-Azure endpoints

When to Use Traffic Manager

- Multi-region deployments with DNS-level failover
- Applications hosted **outside** **Azure**
- DNS-based routing without content acceleration
- **Gradual** **traffic** **shifting** or canary releases
- **Hybrid** **or** **legacy** **apps** that can't use Front Door

---

Traffic Manager Routing Methods

Method	Description
Priority	Failover from primary to backup endpoints
Performance	Routes based on lowest network latency to endpoint
Geographic	Routes users from specific regions to designated endpoints

Weighted	Assign weights to endpoints to distribute load
Multivalue	Returns multiple healthy endpoints
Subnet	Route based on user IP prefix (advanced scenarios)

Example: Performance Routing

A user in Germany is routed to the West Europe endpoint, while a user in the US is routed to East US, based on DNS lookup performance metrics gathered by Microsoft's global monitoring network.

Configuration Example (ARM)

```json
{
  "type": "Microsoft.Network/trafficManagerProfiles",
  "name": "global-traffic-manager",
  "location": "global",
  "properties": {
    "trafficRoutingMethod": "Performance",
    "dnsConfig": {
      "relativeName": "myapp-dns",
      "ttl": 30
    },
    "monitorConfig": {
      "protocol": "HTTP",
      "port": 80,
      "path": "/health"
    },
    "endpoints": [
      {
        "name": "westeurope-endpoint",
        "type":
"Microsoft.Network/trafficManagerProfiles/externalEndpoints",
        "properties": {
          "target": "app-eu.azurewebsites.net",
          "endpointLocation": "West Europe"
        }
      },
      {
```

```
        "name": "eastus-endpoint",
        "type":
"Microsoft.Network/trafficManagerProfiles/externalEndpoints",
        "properties": {
          "target": "app-us.azurewebsites.net",
          "endpointLocation": "East US"
        }
      }
    ]
  }
}
```

Front Door vs. Traffic Manager

Feature	Azure Front Door	Azure Traffic Manager
Layer	Application (L7)	DNS (L3/L4)
Routing granularity	Path, hostname	Region, latency, weight
Protocol awareness	HTTP/HTTPS	All (TCP, UDP, HTTP, etc.)
TLS termination	Yes	No
Health probes	Application-aware	Basic (protocol/path/port)
Endpoint types	Azure and non-Azure	Azure and non-Azure
Global caching/CDN	Yes (Premium)	No
WAF support	Yes	No
Failover speed	Near-instant	DNS TTL dependent

Use **Front Door** for modern web/API workloads and **Traffic Manager** when DNS-level control, hybrid integration, or IP-based routing is required.

Combined Patterns

Many global architectures combine both services:

- **Front Door for application-level routing and performance acceleration**

- **Traffic Manager as a DNS-level failover between regional Front Door endpoints**

- **Azure App Gateway** used behind Front Door for regional WAF policies or TLS inspection

Example architecture:

1. User requests app.contoso.com

2. DNS routes via Traffic Manager to closest regional Front Door

3. Front Door handles SSL, WAF, caching, and L7 routing

4. Routes to regional App Gateway or backend

This offers **defense in depth**, fine-grained routing, and resilient multi-region delivery.

Monitoring and Observability

Azure provides robust tooling for both services:

- **Azure Monitor** for latency, health probe results, traffic volumes

- **Log Analytics** for queryable request logs

- **Alerts** for endpoint health, traffic drops, routing anomalies

Sample Kusto query (Front Door):

```
AzureDiagnostics
| where ResourceType == "FRONTDOORS"
| where httpStatus_d >= 500
| summarize errorCount = count() by clientIP_s, requestUri_s
```

Security Considerations

- **Front** Door
  - Use **WAF rules** to block malicious traffic
  - Enforce **HTTPS-only** access with automatic redirection
  - Restrict access to backends via **Private Link or NSGs**
  - Use **custom domains** with managed certificates
- **Traffic** Manager
  - Secure backend endpoints independently
  - Set short TTLs for faster failover, but be mindful of client DNS caching
  - Use **HTTPS health probes** to ensure app readiness

Best Practices

- Always configure **custom health probes** with a `/health` endpoint to reflect application readiness, not just infrastructure uptime.

- Use **Front Door Premium** for enterprise scenarios that require global WAF and private origin access.

- Combine **Front Door and App Gateway** to balance global and regional routing needs.

- Monitor **backend response times** and use caching or regional replicas to serve content faster.

- Use **staging slots** with Traffic Manager weighted routing for safe production rollouts.

Conclusion

Azure Front Door and Traffic Manager equip architects with the tools needed to build globally resilient and performant applications. Whether you're looking for protocol-aware routing, centralized TLS termination, or DNS-level failover and geofencing, these services enable you to design architectures that meet the demands of modern, globally distributed users.

In the next section, we'll explore hybrid and multi-region network connectivity patterns, including VPN, ExpressRoute, and VNet peering strategies that underpin enterprise-grade architectures.

Designing for Hybrid and Multi-region Connectivity

In today's enterprise cloud architectures, supporting hybrid connectivity (linking on-premises environments with the cloud) and multi-region deployments (serving users and data across different Azure regions) is no longer optional. It is essential for high availability, business continuity, performance optimization, regulatory compliance, and seamless global user experiences.

This section explores the network architecture strategies and Azure services that support hybrid and multi-region connectivity. It includes an in-depth look at Azure VPN Gateway, Azure ExpressRoute, Virtual Network (VNet) peering, Global VNet Peering, Private Link, Network Virtual Appliances (NVAs), and regionally distributed designs using hub-and-spoke topologies.

Core Challenges of Hybrid and Multi-region Networking

Enterprise networking in cloud-native and hybrid environments brings several architectural challenges:

- **Latency-sensitive communication** between regions and sites

- **Security** and **compliance** over untrusted networks

- **Redundancy** and **failover** across geographies

- **Performance bottlenecks** due to poor routing or peering

- **Scalability** of network appliances or transit paths

- **Governance** over distributed infrastructure

Azure addresses these with a comprehensive suite of networking tools, routing strategies, and design patterns.

Azure Virtual Network (VNet)

Every Azure deployment begins with a **Virtual Network**, the fundamental building block of private IP addressing and service isolation.

Key properties:

- Regional scope

- Subnet-based segmentation

- Supports peering, VPN, and Private Link

- Integrated with Azure DNS, NSGs, and route tables

Hybrid Connectivity Options

1. VPN Gateway

Azure VPN Gateway connects on-premises infrastructure to Azure via encrypted tunnels over the public internet.

Types:

- **Site-to-Site VPN**: For branch office or datacenter connectivity

- **Point-to-Site VPN**: For individual client connections (developers, admins)

- **VNet-to-VNet VPN**: For cross-region Azure connectivity

VPN Gateway Configuration Example (Bicep)

```
resource vnet 'Microsoft.Network/virtualNetworks@2022-01-01' = {
  name: 'hybrid-vnet'
  location: resourceGroup().location
  properties: {
    addressSpace: {
      addressPrefixes: [
        '10.1.0.0/16'
      ]
    }
    subnets: [
      {
        name: 'GatewaySubnet'
        properties: {
          addressPrefix: '10.1.255.0/27'
        }
      }
    ]
  }
}
```

```
}

resource vpnGateway 'Microsoft.Network/virtualNetworkGateways@2022-
01-01' = {
  name: 'vpn-gateway'
  location: resourceGroup().location
  properties: {
    ipConfigurations: [
      {
        name: 'gw-ipconfig'
        properties: {
          subnet: {
            id: '${vnet.id}/subnets/GatewaySubnet'
          }
          publicIPAddress: {
            id: publicIp.id
          }
        }
      }
    ]
    gatewayType: 'Vpn'
    vpnType: 'RouteBased'
    enableBgp: false
    sku: {
      name: 'VpnGw2'
    }
  }
}
```

VPN Gateways support bandwidths up to 1.25 Gbps and are ideal for quick hybrid connectivity but have limitations in performance and latency compared to ExpressRoute.

---

2. ExpressRoute

Azure ExpressRoute enables private, high-throughput, and SLA-backed connectivity between Azure and your on-premises networks via a dedicated fiber link.

Key benefits:

- Speeds up to 100 Gbps

- No traffic over the public internet
- Supports Microsoft and private peering
- Integration with ExpressRoute Direct for colocation
- Support for **Global Reach** to interconnect private networks via Azure

ExpressRoute is ideal for:

- Financial institutions requiring private connectivity
- Regulatory workloads (HIPAA, PCI-DSS, FedRAMP)
- Large data transfers (backups, replication)
- Low-latency requirements for hybrid apps

VNet Peering and Global VNet Peering

VNet Peering connects two VNets within the same region using Azure's backbone network. **Global VNet Peering** extends this to different regions.

Characteristics:

- Low-latency, high-bandwidth
- Private IP routing between VNets
- No need for a VPN Gateway
- Supports transitive routing with NVA or hub-and-spoke

Use cases:

- Connecting microservices across VNets
- Multi-region data access
- Shared service access (logging, monitoring, DNS)

Example: Peer a central monitoring VNet to multiple application VNets for centralized observability.

Hub-and-Spoke Topology

A **hub-and-spoke** architecture centralizes connectivity, security, and monitoring, improving governance in complex environments.

- **Hub**: Shared services like firewalls, DNS, bastion, identity
- **Spokes**: Individual application VNets
- **Transitive routing** enabled via NVAs or Azure Route Server

Benefits:

- Reduces management overhead
- Centralized policy enforcement
- Efficient inter-VNet traffic routing
- Scalable multi-region expansion

You can combine this with ExpressRoute or VPN Gateway at the hub for hybrid scenarios.

Azure Route Tables and UDRs

User Defined Routes (UDRs) allow precise control over traffic flow between subnets, VNets, and services.

Examples:

- Force internet-bound traffic through a firewall
- Direct inter-VNet traffic via NVA
- Bypass Azure default system routes

Route table example:

```
{
  "name": "route-to-nva",
  "properties": {
    "routes": [
```

```
    {
      "name": "all-to-nva",
      "properties": {
        "addressPrefix": "0.0.0.0/0",
        "nextHopType": "VirtualAppliance",
        "nextHopIpAddress": "10.1.1.4"
      }
    }
  ]
 }
}
```

Private Link and Private Endpoint

Azure Private Link allows access to Azure PaaS services (e.g., Azure SQL, Blob Storage, Web Apps) via a **private IP address** inside your VNet.

Advantages:

- Eliminates public exposure of services
- Supports VNet NSG, UDR, and integration with hub-spoke
- Secure hybrid and multi-region traffic patterns

Use cases:

- Internal-only access to Cosmos DB or Key Vault
- Enabling cross-region compliance access
- Isolating internal APIs

Private Endpoint + Private DNS Zone is a powerful combination to enforce security and simplify access.

Network Virtual Appliances (NVAs)

NVAs provide enhanced network functionality via third-party or custom appliances.

Common roles:

- Next-gen firewalls (Palo Alto, Fortinet, Cisco)
- VPN concentrators
- SD-WAN gateways
- Deep packet inspection and logging

Place NVAs in the **hub** VNet with UDRs redirecting traffic from spokes through the appliance.

Be mindful of:

- Performance bottlenecks
- Stateful failover configurations
- Scaling via Load Balancer or VMSS

Multi-region Design Patterns

1. Active-Passive Region Pairing

- Primary region handles all traffic
- Secondary is cold standby
- Use **Traffic Manager** or **Front Door** to switch during failover
- Replicate data with **geo-redundant storage** or **active geo-replication**

2. Active-Active Deployment

- Both regions serve traffic
- Front Door routes via **performance routing**
- Data synchronized using **Cosmos DB multi-region writes**, **SQL Geo-replication**, etc.
- Use **eventual consistency** or **region-based partitioning**

3. Data Gravity and Compliance

- Deploy services regionally where data must stay in-country
- Use **regional VNets**, **Private Link**, and **Azure Policy** to enforce locality

---

Monitoring and Governance

Use the following tools for hybrid/multi-region visibility:

- **Azure Network Watcher**: Flow logs, IP reachability, topology
- **Connection Monitor**: Cross-region or site-to-site latency and availability
- **Azure Firewall logs**: Analyze allowed/denied traffic
- **Azure Policy**: Enforce configurations like required NSGs, route tables, private endpoints

Example KQL to detect failed VPN tunnels:

```
AzureDiagnostics
| where Category == "GatewayDiagnosticLog"
| where OperationName == "TunnelDisconnected"
| summarize count() by bin(TimeGenerated, 5m), GatewayName
```

Security Considerations

- Use **NSGs and ASGs** to restrict traffic between services
- Apply **Azure Firewall** or NVAs for deep packet inspection
- Always enable **Diagnostics Logs** for all networking resources
- Enforce **Private Link** for accessing PaaS services
- Use **Azure Defender for Cloud** to evaluate hybrid network posture

---

Best Practices

Area	Best Practice
Hybrid Connectivity	Prefer ExpressRoute over VPN for enterprise workloads
Routing	Centralize UDRs and DNS in hub VNet
VNet Peering	Use Global VNet Peering for cross-region microservice traffic
Private Access	Always enable Private Link for PaaS service connections
Multi-region	Design for eventual consistency unless strong consistency is needed
Governance	Apply Azure Policy to enforce route tables, NSGs, and naming

Conclusion

Designing for hybrid and multi-region connectivity is essential for building resilient, secure, and performant cloud applications in Azure. By leveraging Azure VPN Gateway, ExpressRoute, VNet Peering, hub-and-spoke topology, and Private Link, architects can ensure seamless communication between on-premises infrastructure, regional Azure deployments, and globally distributed services.

When integrated with observability, policy enforcement, and layered security, these network designs lay the foundation for enterprise-grade, cloud-first environments that are ready to meet evolving demands. In the next chapter, we'll shift focus to security, governance, and compliance strategies to scale securely in Azure.

Chapter 7: Scaling Securely: Identity, Governance, and Compliance

Azure AD for Multi-Tenant and Scalable Identity

As cloud-native applications and enterprise systems scale globally, managing identity becomes a central concern for security, user experience, and regulatory compliance. Azure Active Directory (Azure AD) serves as the identity backbone of Microsoft's cloud ecosystem. It provides a powerful, scalable, and secure platform for managing users, applications, and access—supporting everything from single-tenant enterprises to massive multi-tenant SaaS solutions.

This section explores how to design and implement identity strategies using Azure AD that support scale, ensure isolation, and provide centralized control. Topics include single-tenant vs. multi-tenant models, external identities, federation, B2B/B2C integrations, conditional access, and identity lifecycle management in modern cloud architecture.

Identity as a Pillar of Cloud Security

Identity is the new perimeter in cloud-native systems. In a world without traditional network boundaries, every request must be authenticated and authorized based on **who** is making the request, **what** they are trying to access, and **where** they are coming from.

Azure AD serves as the central identity provider across:

- Microsoft 365 and SaaS services
- Azure infrastructure and PaaS services
- Enterprise applications (custom and 3rd-party)
- External user collaboration (B2B)
- Customer-facing authentication (B2C)

Single-Tenant vs. Multi-Tenant Identity Models

Azure AD supports both **single-tenant** and **multi-tenant** application models. Choosing the right model affects scalability, security, and tenant management.

Single-Tenant Model

- App registered and only available to users in the same Azure AD tenant
- Used for internal enterprise apps
- Full control over users, policies, and consent

Use case: Internal HR portal used only by employees in `contoso.com`.

Multi-Tenant Model

- App is registered in one tenant but can be used by users from any Azure AD tenant
- Consent is managed via OAuth2 flows
- Requires tenant isolation logic in app

Use case: A SaaS CRM platform serving thousands of B2B customers.

Multi-tenant applications require careful design for:

- Tenant-aware user routing
- Tenant-specific configuration and policies
- Data isolation at the application and database levels

Registering Multi-Tenant Applications

Azure AD uses **app registrations** and **service principals** to enable access across tenants.

```
{
  "appId": "XXXXXXXX-XXXX-XXXX-XXXX-XXXXXXXXXXXX",
  "publisherDomain": "saascompany.com",
  "signInAudience": "AzureADMultipleOrgs"
}
```

Steps:

1. Register the app in your home tenant.
2. Set signInAudience to AzureADMultipleOrgs.

3. Configure permissions (Microsoft Graph, custom scopes).

4. Handle consent (admin/user) via login flow.

External Identities and B2B Collaboration

Azure AD B2B enables organizations to collaborate securely with external partners by inviting them as guest users.

Key capabilities:

- Guests use their existing credentials (Google, Microsoft, etc.).

- Access governed by host tenant's policies.

- Supports entitlement management and governance.

Benefits:

- Centralized identity platform

- Secure onboarding/offboarding

- Granular access control (RBAC + Conditional Access)

Example: A supplier is invited to `contoso.com` and assigned access to SharePoint and a custom logistics app.

Inviting Guests Programmatically (PowerShell)

```
New-AzureADMSInvitation                     -InvitedUserEmailAddress
"partner@othercompany.com" `
  -InviteRedirectUrl "https://portal.contoso.com/welcome" `
  -SendInvitationMessage $true
```

Azure AD B2C for Customer Identity

Azure AD B2C (Business to Consumer) is a separate service designed for public-facing apps with massive scale and custom branding.

Key features:

- Social identity providers (Facebook, Google, LinkedIn)

- Local accounts with email/SMS verification

- Custom UI/UX with HTML, CSS, JavaScript

- Policy engine (user journeys, API integration)

- MFA and Conditional Access support

Use case: E-commerce platform supporting millions of customer accounts across regions.

B2C scales to **hundreds of millions of identities**, with flexible policies to support account recovery, sign-up flows, terms of use, and multifactor workflows.

Conditional Access and Risk-Based Policies

Azure AD Conditional Access enables dynamic access control based on real-time signals.

Conditions:

- User/group membership

- Device state (compliant, hybrid-joined)

- Application being accessed

- Location or IP

- Risk level (sign-in risk, user risk)

Controls:

- Require MFA

- Block access

- Require compliant device

- Require password change

Example Policy:

If:

```
  - User in "Engineering"
  - Accessing from Untrusted Location
Then:
  - Require MFA
```

Combine Conditional Access with **Identity Protection** to automatically block or alert on risky sign-ins.

Role-Based Access Control (RBAC) in Azure AD

Azure RBAC allows you to control access to Azure resources using roles assigned to users, groups, service principals, and managed identities.

Key built-in roles:

- Owner – Full management access

- Contributor – Manage everything but no access control

- Reader – View only

- User Access Administrator – Manage user access

Use **custom roles** for fine-grained control over sensitive operations.

Example role assignment using Azure CLI:

```
az role assignment create \
  --assignee user@contoso.com \
  --role "Reader" \
  --scope "/subscriptions/xxxx/resourceGroups/my-rg"
```

Managed Identities for Applications

Azure provides **Managed Identities** to eliminate the need for app secrets and credentials.

Types:

- **System-assigned**: Tied to a single resource

- **User-assigned**: Can be shared across resources

Use cases:

- Azure Functions accessing Key Vault
- AKS workloads needing to authenticate to Azure services
- App Services retrieving configuration from App Configuration

Example usage with Azure SDK (Python):

```python
from azure.identity import DefaultAzureCredential
from azure.keyvault.secrets import SecretClient

credential = DefaultAzureCredential()
client = SecretClient(vault_url="https://myvault.vault.azure.net/",
credential=credential)
secret = client.get_secret("DbConnectionString")
```

Identity Lifecycle Management

Key components for managing identity lifecycle:

- **Azure AD Connect**: Syncs on-premises AD users to Azure AD
- **Group-based licensing**: Automate app and license assignment
- **Access reviews**: Periodic validation of access rights
- **Entitlement management**: Automate onboarding/offboarding

Enable governance at scale by using **Microsoft Entra Identity Governance** for workflows and policy enforcement.

Multi-Tenant Architecture Patterns

In a SaaS platform serving multiple customers (tenants), identity design must enforce:

1. **Tenant-aware login flows** (e.g., domain suffix detection)
2. **Authorization boundaries** between tenants (RBAC or ABAC)

3. **Per-tenant branding and settings** (stored in DB or config)

4. **Auditing and analytics** scoped per tenant

5. **Tenant provisioning and consent management**

Example login URL:

```
https://login.microsoftonline.com/common/oauth2/v2.0/authorize?
client_id=YOUR_APP_ID
&response_type=code
&redirect_uri=https://app.saas.com/callback
&scope=openid profile email
&prompt=consent
```

In the token, `tid` (tenant ID) identifies the organization. Use it to map to internal configuration and enforce data segregation.

Best Practices

Area	Best Practice
Identity Isolation	Use multi-tenant app model with per-tenant data and access control
Consent Management	Use admin consent flows to avoid user sprawl
Federation	Federate with existing IDPs where possible (SAML, OIDC)
Guest Access	Restrict guest permissions via Conditional Access and PIM
Governance	Automate reviews, enforce MFA, track risky sign-ins
Secretless Auth	Use Managed Identities to eliminate credentials
Monitoring	Enable sign-in logs, audit logs, and alerting for anomalies

---

Conclusion

Azure Active Directory is central to enabling secure and scalable identity in the cloud. Whether you're supporting internal enterprise users, external collaborators, or millions of customers, Azure AD provides the tools to build identity-first architectures that align with Zero Trust principles and regulatory mandates.

By combining Azure AD, B2B/B2C, Conditional Access, RBAC, and managed identities, architects can create secure, tenant-aware solutions that scale with confidence—while maintaining governance, transparency, and user experience at every layer.

In the next section, we'll extend this discussion to Role-Based Access Control and policy management for enforcing granular, automated, and scalable security posture across your Azure environment.

Role-Based Access Control (RBAC) and Policy Management

As organizations scale their Azure environments, managing access becomes a foundational security requirement. It is essential not only to enforce the principle of least privilege but also to establish clear boundaries around who can do what, where, and under what conditions. Azure provides two powerful governance tools to achieve this: **Role-Based Access Control (RBAC)** and **Azure Policy**.

RBAC governs **who** can perform actions on Azure resources, while Azure Policy governs **what** actions and configurations are allowed. Together, they form the cornerstone of secure and compliant Azure architecture.

Understanding RBAC in Azure

RBAC is an authorization system that provides fine-grained access control over Azure resources. It uses **roles** and **assignments** to allow or deny actions based on the user's identity and scope of access.

Key Concepts

- **Security principal**: A user, group, service principal, or managed identity.

- **Role definition**: A collection of permissions (read, write, delete).

- **Scope**: The boundary of access — subscription, resource group, or resource.

- **Role assignment**: The act of binding a role to a principal at a scope.

Example hierarchy:

Subscription

```
└── Resource Group
     └── Resource (e.g., VM, Storage Account)
```

Roles assigned at a **higher level** inherit down unless overridden.

Built-in Role Examples

Role Name	Description
Owner	Full access, including assigning roles
Contributor	Manage resources but cannot assign roles
Reader	View only
Virtual Machine Contributor	Manage VMs but not virtual networks
Storage Blob Data Reader	Read-only access to blob storage data

Azure also supports **custom roles** for more granular control.

Creating a Custom Role (ARM Example)

```
{
  "Name": "Virtual Network Operator",
  "IsCustom": true,
  "Description": "Can manage virtual networks, but not gateways",
  "Actions": [
    "Microsoft.Network/virtualNetworks/*",
    "Microsoft.Resources/subscriptions/resourceGroups/read"
  ],
  "NotActions": [
    "Microsoft.Network/virtualNetworkGateways/*"
  ],
  "AssignableScopes": [
    "/subscriptions/{subscription-id}"
  ]
```

```
}
```

Assign custom roles using the Azure CLI:

```
az role definition create --role-definition ./vnetOperatorRole.json
```

RBAC Assignment via Azure CLI

```
az role assignment create \
  --assignee "jane@contoso.com" \
  --role "Reader" \
  --scope "/subscriptions/xxxx/resourceGroups/my-rg"
```

This gives the user read-only access to resources in the my-rg resource group.

Best Practices for RBAC

1. **Use groups, not individuals**: Assign roles to groups in Azure AD for easier management.

2. **Follow least privilege**: Give only the permissions necessary for the job.

3. **Use custom roles when needed**: Tailor access to match operational models.

4. **Review assignments regularly**: Use Azure Governance tools for periodic reviews.

5. **Avoid overuse of Owner role**: Reserve for administrators with full accountability.

Azure Policy Overview

While RBAC controls actions, **Azure Policy** enforces and audits resource configurations. It allows organizations to define rules that resources must comply with, helping maintain security, compliance, and operational standards at scale.

What Azure Policy Can Do

- Enforce   resource   tagging

- Restrict locations for resource deployments
- Control VM SKUs or allowed sizes
- Audit or deny public IP addresses on VMs
- Require diagnostics to be enabled on all resources
- Enforce naming conventions

Components of Azure Policy

- **Policy definition**: JSON rule describing the condition and effect
- **Initiative (policy set)**: A group of related policies
- **Assignment**: Applying a policy or initiative to a scope

Policy scopes can be **management group**, **subscription**, **resource group**, or **individual resource**.

Policy Definition Example

Enforce resources to be deployed only in East US or West Europe:

```
{
  "if": {
    "not": {
      "field": "location",
      "in": ["eastus", "westeurope"]
    }
  },
  "then": {
    "effect": "deny"
  }
}
```

Assignment via Bicep:

```
resource                                    policyAssignment
'Microsoft.Authorization/policyAssignments@2021-06-01' = {
  name: 'enforce-location'
  properties: {
    policyDefinitionId:
'/providers/Microsoft.Authorization/policyDefinitions/EnforceLocatio
n'
    scope: subscription().id
  }
}
```

Common Policy Effects

Effect	Description
Deny	Prevents non-compliant resources from being created
Audit	Flags non-compliant resources but allows deployment
Append	Adds specified fields to the resource request
Modify	Changes the request to conform with policy (e.g., add tag)
DeployIfNotExists	Automatically deploys needed resources if they don't exist

Use **DeployIfNotExists** to enforce monitoring agents, security baselines, or backups.

Initiatives: Grouping Policies

Policies can be grouped into initiatives to manage compliance at scale.

Example: "Production Resource Compliance" initiative could include:

- Only deploy to allowed regions
- Require tags: env, owner
- Enforce diagnostics settings

- Disallow public IPs

```json
{
  "name": "prod-resource-initiative",
  "policyDefinitions": [
    { "policyDefinitionId": "/policies/location-enforcement" },
    { "policyDefinitionId": "/policies/require-tags" },
    { "policyDefinitionId": "/policies/no-public-ip" }
  ]
}
```

Monitoring Policy Compliance

Azure Policy integrates with **Azure Monitor** and **Compliance Dashboard** in the Azure Portal.

- View non-compliant resources
- Drill into assignment scope
- Remediate via **remediation** **tasks**
- Export to **Log** **Analytics** for custom reporting

Example KQL for finding non-compliant VMs:

```kql
PolicyResources
| where PolicyAssignmentName contains "prod-resource-initiative"
| where ComplianceState == "NonCompliant"
| where ResourceType == "microsoft.compute/virtualmachines"
```

Policy + RBAC: Enforcement and Access Control

Use **RBAC to control actions** and **Policy to control configurations**.

Scenario:

- Developers can deploy VMs (RBAC)
- But VMs must be in eastus, have tag env=dev, and disallow public IPs (Policy)

This separation of concerns creates **governance boundaries** between access and compliance.

Azure Blueprints (Optional Legacy Integration)

Azure Blueprints enable packaging RBAC, policies, ARM templates, and resource groups into repeatable, versioned deployments.

However, Blueprints are being deprecated in favor of **Template Specs** and **Policy as Code (PaC)** practices using tools like **Terraform**, **Bicep**, and **Azure DevOps Pipelines**.

Still, they offer a good starting point for **landing zones**, especially in highly regulated environments.

Automating with Policy as Code

Use GitOps or DevOps pipelines to define and enforce policies declaratively.

- Store policy definitions in source control
- Use **Terraform** or **Bicep** to apply policies and RBAC assignments
- Automate compliance reporting and remediation
- Integrate with **Azure Lighthouse** for cross-tenant governance

This enables **auditable, repeatable, and scalable** policy enforcement.

Best Practices for RBAC and Policy

Area	Recommendation
RBAC	Assign roles to groups, not users
Least Privilege	Use built-in or custom roles scoped narrowly
Policy	Start with `Audit` before moving to `Deny`
Naming	Use consistent naming conventions for assignments

Compliance	Regularly review compliance reports and automate remediation
Segmentation	Use management groups to scope policies across environments
Automation	Embed RBAC/Policy in CI/CD and IaC pipelines
Reporting	Use Azure Monitor + Log Analytics to track violations

Conclusion

Role-Based Access Control and Azure Policy are essential to scaling securely in Azure. RBAC ensures the right people and services have the right level of access at the right scope, while Azure Policy ensures that resources meet organizational standards and compliance requirements.

Together, they empower architects to balance agility with control—enabling innovation without sacrificing security or governance. In the next section, we'll explore how to create enterprise-scale governance frameworks using Azure Blueprints, landing zones, and automated guardrails.

Governance with Azure Blueprints and Landing Zones

As organizations adopt cloud at scale, the challenge shifts from individual resource provisioning to consistent, secure, and compliant **governance** across the enterprise. Managing thousands of subscriptions, enforcing policies, ensuring regulatory alignment, and empowering development teams without compromising on guardrails becomes essential.

Azure Blueprints and **Landing Zones** are central to this effort. They provide pre-configured templates for deploying compliant, secure, and standardized Azure environments. Whether you're building a new line-of-business app or onboarding an entire department to Azure, these tools allow you to scale governance with confidence.

The Need for Governance at Scale

Traditional IT governance relied on manual controls, ticket-based workflows, and centralized teams. In the cloud, where resources can be deployed in seconds, manual processes no longer scale. Instead, modern governance must be:

- **Automated**: Defined as code and enforced programmatically.

- **Repeatable**: Applied consistently across all environments.

- **Scoped**: Flexible enough to vary by team, department, or region.

- **Measurable**: Tracked and audited continuously for compliance.

Governance ensures that cloud adoption remains aligned with security, financial, operational, and organizational goals.

What Are Azure Blueprints?

Azure Blueprints allow you to **orchestrate the deployment of resource templates, RBAC roles, policies, and resources** across subscriptions and management groups.

Components of a Blueprint:

- **Artifacts**: The individual items included in a blueprint. These can be:

  - **Policy**   **Assignments**

  - **Role**   **Assignments**

  - **ARM**   **Templates**   **(or**   **Bicep)**

  - **Resource**   **Groups**

- **Blueprint Definition**: The collection of artifacts and parameters that define a blueprint.

- **Blueprint Assignment**: Deploys the blueprint to a specific scope (subscription or management group).

Blueprints can be **versioned** and **locked**, ensuring consistent environments and preventing unauthorized changes.

Common Blueprint Use Cases

- Creating **Landing Zones** for dev/test/prod environments.

- Enforcing **compliance** with internal standards or external regulations (e.g., ISO 27001, HIPAA).

- Rapidly **onboarding new teams or business units** with predefined configurations.

- Establishing **guardrails** to prevent misconfigurations or security risks.

Example: A Finance blueprint may include:

- Resource group structure for compute, storage, and networking

- Policy to allow only East US and West Europe regions

- Logging and diagnostics settings

- Role assignments for finance ops team

- Encryption settings for all data services

Landing Zones: Foundation for Scalable Azure Environments

A **Landing Zone** is a pre-configured Azure environment that includes the foundational resources and configurations needed to deploy workloads securely and at scale.

Landing zones often include:

- Network topology (hub-and-spoke, firewalls, NSGs)

- Identity integration (Azure AD, RBAC)

- Monitoring and diagnostics (Log Analytics, alerts)

- Security and policy enforcement

- DevOps pipelines

- Budgeting and cost management settings

Microsoft provides **Cloud Adoption Framework (CAF)** landing zone reference implementations that cover everything from MVP (minimum viable product) environments to enterprise-scale architectures.

Enterprise-Scale Landing Zones

The **Enterprise-Scale** architecture in Azure is a validated, opinionated approach to organizing Azure resources for large enterprises. It provides:

- A **modular architecture** with flexible deployment options

- **Management group hierarchy** for role and policy inheritance
- Support for **multiple subscriptions per workload**
- Integration with **Azure Policy**, **Azure Blueprints**, and **Resource Graph**

Example management group hierarchy:

```
Root
├── Platform
│   ├── Connectivity
│   └── Identity
└── LandingZones
    ├── Corp
    └── Online
```

This structure allows for clear separation of roles, policies, and resources across business units and workloads.

Azure Blueprint Example Definition (JSON)

```json
{
  "properties": {
    "description": "Standard Landing Zone for Development",
    "targetScope": "subscription",
    "parameters": {},
    "resourceGroups": {
      "networking": {
        "name": "networking-rg",
        "location": "eastus"
      },
      "compute": {
        "name": "compute-rg",
        "location": "eastus"
      }
    },
    "policyAssignments": [
      {
```

```
        "policyDefinitionId":
"/providers/Microsoft.Authorization/policyDefinitions/allowed-
locations",
        "parameters": {
          "listOfAllowedLocations": {
            "value": ["eastus", "westeurope"]
          }
        }
      }
    ],
    "roleAssignments": [
      {
        "roleDefinitionId":
"/providers/Microsoft.Authorization/roleDefinitions/contributor-
role-id",
        "principalIds": ["object-id-of-devops-group"]
      }
    ],
    "template": {
      "$schema":  "https://schema.management.azure.com/schemas/2019-
04-01/deploymentTemplate.json#",
      "contentVersion": "1.0.0.0",
      "resources": []
    }
  }
}
```

Assigning a blueprint with CLI:

```
az blueprint assignment create \
  --name dev-landing-zone \
  --blueprint-name dev-blueprint \
  --location eastus \
  --subscription {subscriptionId}
```

Transition to Template Specs

Azure Blueprints is being deprecated in favor of **Template Specs**, which allow you to store and version ARM or Bicep templates natively in Azure.

Template Specs can be combined with:

- Azure Policy (for enforcement)
- Azure DevOps or GitHub Actions (for automation)
- Role assignments via IaC

This shift aligns with Infrastructure as Code best practices and integrates better with CI/CD workflows.

Governance Automation and Guardrails

Key governance patterns include:

1. **Policy-as-Code**: Store all policies in source control, deploy via pipelines.
2. **RBAC-as-Code**: Define role assignments using Bicep or Terraform.
3. **Subscription Vending**: Use automation to deploy landing zones to new subscriptions.
4. **Resource Locks**: Protect critical resources from accidental deletion (CanNotDelete).

Example Bicep Template for Landing Zone

```
module networking 'modules/networking.bicep' = {
  name: 'deploy-networking'
  params: {
    location: 'eastus'
  }
}

resource rg 'Microsoft.Resources/resourceGroups@2021-04-01' = {
  name: 'compute-rg'
  location: 'eastus'
}

resource                                     diagnosticSetting
'Microsoft.Insights/diagnosticSettings@2021-05-01-preview' = {
  name: 'audit-logs'
  scope: rg
```

```
  properties: {
    workspaceId: logAnalytics.id
    logs: [
      {
        category: 'AuditLogs'
        enabled: true
      }
    ]
  }
}
```

This template can be integrated into a landing zone pipeline that enforces logging, access control, and network policies automatically.

Monitoring and Compliance

Use **Azure Policy Compliance Dashboard** to view:

- Non-compliant   resources

- Remediation   actions   needed

- Assignment   history   and   changes

Integrate with **Azure Resource Graph** to query large environments:

```
PolicyResources
| where ComplianceState == 'NonCompliant'
| summarize count() by PolicyAssignmentName
```

Audit trail and version control can be achieved using **GitOps workflows** and change control pipelines.

Best Practices

Category	Practice
Governance	Define landing zones per business unit or workload

Automation	Use Template Specs or Bicep + Azure DevOps/GitHub for repeatable deployment
Policy Control	Enforce security, location, and tagging policies at management group
Role Assignment	Use Azure AD groups + scoped custom roles
Compliance	Track non-compliance and remediate regularly
Documentation	Maintain blueprints and landing zone configs in version-controlled repos

Conclusion

Azure Blueprints and Landing Zones are key tools for enabling governance at scale. They allow organizations to accelerate Azure adoption without sacrificing control, security, or compliance. By predefining infrastructure, policy, and access control configurations, teams can deploy consistent environments aligned with corporate standards.

As organizations evolve, transitioning toward Template Specs and full Infrastructure as Code models will provide even greater agility, traceability, and automation. In the next chapter, we'll explore how to operationalize observability with Azure Monitor, Log Analytics, and automated alerting frameworks to maintain operational excellence in cloud-native applications.

Chapter 8: Observability and Operational Excellence

Designing for Monitoring with Azure Monitor and Log Analytics

Modern cloud applications demand more than just high availability and scalability—they require **deep visibility** into their internal state and external behavior to ensure performance, reliability, compliance, and cost control. Observability is not a luxury or afterthought; it is a foundational design principle in cloud-native architecture.

In Azure, the key services for building observability are **Azure Monitor** and **Log Analytics**. Together, they form a comprehensive telemetry and analytics platform that captures metrics, logs, traces, and insights across every layer of the stack—from infrastructure to applications, databases, networks, and even security controls.

This section explores how to architect applications and environments with observability built-in from the start, how to use Azure Monitor and Log Analytics effectively, and how to establish proactive alerting, visualization, and correlation strategies that scale with your environment.

The Pillars of Observability

Observability in cloud-native systems is built on three core pillars:

1. **Metrics**: Numeric values that describe the state of a system (e.g., CPU usage, request rate, latency).

2. **Logs**: Timestamped records of events, warnings, errors, and custom application messages.

3. **Traces**: Distributed tracking of request flow across services, useful for debugging and performance analysis.

Azure Monitor supports all three pillars and integrates with other Azure services and third-party observability tools like Grafana, Elastic Stack, and Prometheus.

What Is Azure Monitor?

Azure Monitor is the umbrella service for all monitoring and telemetry capabilities in Azure. It provides:

- Metrics collection and aggregation
- Log collection and querying via Log Analytics
- Distributed tracing through Application Insights
- Alerting and action groups
- Dashboards and workbooks
- Autoscale integration
- Service Health notifications
- Export to Event Hubs, Storage, and SIEM tools

Azure Monitor is deeply integrated with virtually every Azure resource, allowing you to capture telemetry from the control plane, data plane, infrastructure, and application layers.

Log Analytics Workspace

Log Analytics is the data engine behind Azure Monitor logs. It stores and indexes logs collected from:

- Azure resources (e.g., VMs, App Services, Key Vaults)
- Azure Monitor metrics and diagnostic logs
- On-premises agents and custom apps
- Application Insights telemetry

Logs are stored in a **Log Analytics Workspace**, which supports:

- Role-based access control
- Data retention policies
- Advanced Kusto Query Language (KQL) queries
- Workbooks and alerts

Log Analytics enables centralized observability across subscriptions, tenants, or environments.

Instrumenting Resources for Monitoring

1. Azure Resource Monitoring

Most Azure resources expose diagnostic settings that allow telemetry to be sent to:

- Log   Analytics

- Storage   account

- Event   Hub

Example: Enabling diagnostics for an Azure App Service

```
az monitor diagnostic-settings create \
  --name "app-logs" \
  --resource                "/subscriptions/xxxx/resourceGroups/my-
rg/providers/Microsoft.Web/sites/myapp" \
  --workspace               "/subscriptions/xxxx/resourcegroups/logs-
rg/providers/microsoft.operationalinsights/workspaces/myworkspace" \
  --logs '[{"category": "AppServiceHTTPLogs", "enabled": true}]' \
  --metrics '[{"category": "AllMetrics", "enabled": true}]'
```

You can also automate this using **Bicep**, **ARM**, or **Terraform**.

2. Application Monitoring with Application Insights

Application Insights is the APM (Application Performance Monitoring) component of Azure Monitor. It provides:

- Request   and   dependency   tracking

- Exception   logging

- User   and   session   analytics

- Custom   telemetry

- Live   metrics   and   snapshots

Integrate via SDKs in .NET, Node.js, Java, Python, or by using the **auto-instrumentation agent** in App Service, AKS, or Azure Functions.

Example in .NET:

```
services.AddApplicationInsightsTelemetry(Configuration["APPINSIGHTS_
INSTRUMENTATIONKEY"]);
```

App Insights supports **sampling**, **export**, and **retention** configuration to manage volume and cost.

Kusto Query Language (KQL)

KQL is a powerful language used in Log Analytics to query and analyze telemetry data.

Example 1: Failed Requests Over Time

```
requests
| where success == false
| summarize count() by bin(timestamp, 5m), resultCode
```

Example 2: Top Error Messages

```
exceptions
| summarize count() by type, outerMessage
| top 10 by count_
```

Example 3: CPU Usage on VMs

```
Perf
| where ObjectName == "Processor" and CounterName == "% Processor
Time"
| summarize avg(CounterValue) by bin(TimeGenerated, 5m), Computer
```

KQL supports joins, regex, aggregation, time-binning, and cross-workspace queries.

Alerts and Action Groups

Monitoring without alerting is incomplete. Azure Monitor allows you to define **metric-based** or **log-based** alerts.

Types:

- **Metric   Alerts:**   Near-real-time,   low-latency   triggers

- **Log Alerts**: Advanced, cross-resource queries

- **Activity Log Alerts**: Based on Azure control plane actions

- **Service Health Alerts**: Based on Azure service-level disruptions

Action Groups support:

- Email/SMS/Push notifications

- Azure Function or Logic App triggers

- Webhook calls

- ITSM integrations (e.g., ServiceNow)

Example: Alert when CPU > 80% on any VM

```
az monitor metrics alert create \
  --name "HighCPUAlert" \
  --resource                "/subscriptions/xxxx/resourceGroups/my-
rg/providers/Microsoft.Compute/virtualMachines/myvm" \
  --condition "avg Percentage CPU > 80" \
  --description "Alert when CPU exceeds 80%" \
  --action-group myActionGroup
```

Workbooks and Dashboards

Azure Workbooks are interactive, query-driven reports that combine metrics, logs, parameters, and visualizations. They can be used for:

- Executive dashboards

- DevOps insights

- Security and compliance overviews

- SLA tracking

Workbooks support charts, grids, markdown, custom parameters, and KQL queries.

Example use case: Application health dashboard with request latency, error rate, and user count, filtered by environment or region.

Designing for Observability

Observability must be **architected**, not bolted on. Key design considerations:

- **Define telemetry strategy** early in the design process
- **Tag resources** with environment, owner, app name for filtered monitoring
- **Isolate logs** per environment but aggregate at the enterprise level
- **Standardize diagnostics** using policies or CI/CD pipelines
- **Instrument custom code** for business-level insights (e.g., basket size, checkout duration)

Cost Management

Observability comes with a cost. To manage it:

- Use **data caps** on Log Analytics ingestion
- Apply **retention policies** (e.g., 30/90/180 days)
- Sample high-volume telemetry in App Insights
- Aggregate metrics before export (reduce granularity)
- Use **dedicated** or **capacity-based pricing** for large environments

Governance and Access Control

Control access to monitoring data with:

- **RBAC roles** (Log Analytics Reader, Monitoring Contributor)
- **Data collection rules (DCRs)** for granular data source control
- **Azure Policy** to enforce diagnostic settings

Example Policy: Require all VMs to send logs to a central workspace

```
{
  "if": {
    "field": "type",
    "equals": "Microsoft.Compute/virtualMachines"
  },
  "then": {
    "effect": "deployIfNotExists",
    "details": {
      "type": "Microsoft.Insights/diagnosticSettings",
      "existenceCondition": {
        "field":
"Microsoft.Insights/diagnosticSettings/logAnalytics.destinationType"
,
        "equals": "Dedicated"
      }
    }
  }
}
```

Integration with Third-Party Tools

Azure Monitor supports integration with:

• **SIEMs**	like	Splunk,	Sentinel,	Elastic
• **Grafana**	dashboards	(native	Azure	plugin)
• **Prometheus**	via	Azure	Monitor	for	containers
• **Datadog**	and	New	Relic	via	agents

This allows hybrid monitoring across cloud and on-premises systems.

Best Practices

Area	Best Practice
Instrumentation	Start with App Insights or Diagnostic Settings for every service

Centralization	Use a shared Log Analytics workspace per environment or region
Automation	Include monitoring setup in Bicep/Terraform/ARM pipelines
Visualization	Build Workbooks for application, infra, and security metrics
Alerting	Prioritize high-value, actionable alerts only
Retention	Align retention with compliance needs and budget
Access	Grant RBAC to logs/dashboards based on app ownership
Scaling	Use dedicated ingestion tiers or sampling for large environments

Conclusion

Observability is the bedrock of operational excellence in cloud-native systems. With Azure Monitor and Log Analytics, you can architect systems that are transparent, traceable, and resilient from day one. By embedding metrics, logs, and traces into the core of your application and infrastructure design, you empower your teams to detect anomalies faster, resolve incidents proactively, and drive continuous improvement based on data.

In the next section, we'll explore how performance tuning and cost optimization practices can be integrated into your architecture to ensure that your Azure workloads not only scale effectively but also operate efficiently.

Performance Tuning and Cost Optimization

Cloud computing offers unprecedented scalability and agility, but these benefits can come at a cost—both financially and in terms of application performance if not carefully managed. In Azure, performance tuning and cost optimization are not just engineering concerns; they are architectural responsibilities. To deliver sustainable and efficient solutions, architects must design with performance and cost in mind from the beginning.

This section provides a deep dive into strategies, tools, and patterns for tuning application performance and reducing cloud expenditure. From infrastructure and networking to databases, storage, and monitoring, we'll cover how to measure, assess, and optimize systems holistically across your Azure estate.

The Dual Mandate: Performance vs. Cost

The goal of performance tuning is to ensure that applications respond quickly and scale predictably under load. Cost optimization aims to deliver that performance without waste or overspending. Often, these goals appear at odds—higher performance usually costs more—but in cloud-native systems, the right architecture achieves both.

Focus	Performance Goal	Cost Optimization Goal
Compute	Low latency, high throughput	Right-size VMs, scale on demand
Storage	Fast read/write operations	Use appropriate storage tiers
Database	Efficient queries, concurrency	Optimize indexes, reduce DTUs/RUs
Network	Low-latency, high-bandwidth connectivity	Avoid data egress fees, right-size traffic
Monitoring	Granular, real-time metrics	Limit retention, sample telemetry

Balancing these goals requires continuous measurement and iteration.

Right-Sizing Compute Resources

Many workloads use **over-provisioned** virtual machines or App Service Plans that drive unnecessary cost.

Key Tactics

1. **Use Azure Advisor** to identify underutilized VMs.

2. **Monitor CPU, memory, and disk IOPS** via Azure Monitor metrics.

3. **Select the right VM series** (e.g., B-series for bursty workloads, E-series for memory-intensive tasks).

4. **Leverage autoscaling** in App Services, VMSS, and AKS.

Example: App Service Plan autoscale rule (CPU > 75%):

```
az monitor autoscale create \
  --resource
"/subscriptions/xxxx/resourceGroups/rg/providers/Microsoft.Web/serve
rfarms/myappplan" \
```

```
  --name "autoscale-cpu" \
  --min-count 2 \
  --max-count 10 \
  --count 2

az monitor autoscale rule create \
  --resource
"/subscriptions/xxxx/resourceGroups/rg/providers/Microsoft.Web/serve
rfarms/myappplan" \
  --condition "CpuPercentage > 75 avg 5m" \
  --scale out 1
```

Reserved Instances and Spot VMs

- **Reserved Instances (RIs)**: Commit to 1–3 year VM usage for up to 72% savings.

- **Spot VMs**: Use spare capacity for non-critical or interruptible workloads.

Optimizing Storage and Data Access

Storage can have a significant impact on both performance and cost, especially in data-intensive applications.

Strategies

1. **Use the right storage tier**:

   - Premium SSD for low-latency

   - Standard HDD for infrequent access

   - Archive for long-term retention

2. **Enable blob tiering**:

   - Automatically move data to cooler tiers using lifecycle management policies.

3. **Avoid unnecessary data duplication**:

   - Use shared access and snapshots.

4. **Cache reads with Azure Cache for Redis**:

- Reduce IOPS and improve response time.

Example Bicep lifecycle policy for hot-to-cool transition:

```
resource storageAccount 'Microsoft.Storage/storageAccounts@2022-09-
01' = {
  name: 'mystorageacct'
  location: 'eastus'
  sku: { name: 'Standard_GRS' }
  kind: 'StorageV2'
  properties: {
    accessTier: 'Hot'
    allowBlobPublicAccess: false
  }
}

resource                                                    lifecycle
'Microsoft.Storage/storageAccounts/managementPolicies@2022-09-01'  =
{
  name: 'default'
  parent: storageAccount
  properties: {
    policy: {
      rules: [
        {
          name: 'move-to-cool'
          enabled: true
          type: 'Lifecycle'
          definition: {
            actions: {
              baseBlob: {
                tierToCool: { daysAfterModificationGreaterThan: 30 }
              }
            }
            filters: { blobTypes: ['blockBlob'] }
          }
        }
      ]
    }
  }
}
```

Database Tuning

Databases are often the bottleneck in cloud applications—and one of the costliest components.

Performance Tactics

- **Optimize indexes** to support common queries.
- Use **partitioning** in Cosmos DB and SQL Hyperscale.
- Cache frequent queries (Redis or in-app memory).
- Use **Query Store** and **Automatic Tuning** for SQL Database.

Cost Optimization

- Use **serverless** SQL tier for sporadic workloads.
- Use **elastic pools** to share resources among multiple small databases.
- Tune Cosmos DB throughput:
  - Provisioned RU/s vs. Autoscale
  - Avoid cross-partition queries
  - Monitor hot partitions

Network and Egress Optimization

Azure charges for **data egress**, not ingress. Reducing outbound data volume and optimizing connectivity paths can cut significant cost.

Key Tips

- **Use Azure CDN** to cache static content at the edge.
- Minimize cross-region traffic unless required.
- Leverage **Private Link** to avoid egress charges within VNet.

- Use **Application Gateway** or **Front Door** for intelligent routing and caching.

- Use **ExpressRoute** for large or sensitive data transfers.

Monitoring and Diagnostics Efficiency

Observability tools can generate massive volumes of telemetry. Without proper tuning, you can incur high storage and ingestion costs.

Strategies

- Set **sampling rates** in Application Insights.

- Use **Log Analytics data caps**.

- Apply **diagnostic settings only to necessary categories**.

- Set **retention policies** (e.g., 30 days for dev, 180 for prod).

- Aggregate metrics instead of raw logs for long-term storage.

Example: Set retention policy for Log Analytics workspace to 60 days:

```
az monitor log-analytics workspace update \
  --resource-group logs-rg \
  --workspace-name myworkspace \
  --retention-time 60
```

Using Azure Advisor

Azure Advisor provides **personalized recommendations** for:

- Cost savings

- High availability

- Security improvements

- Operational excellence

- Performance

Integrate Azure Advisor findings into CI/CD or governance dashboards to automate optimization enforcement.

Example categories:

```
az advisor recommendation list --category Cost
```

Exporting to CSV or monitoring system allows you to track progress over time.

Azure Cost Management + Budgets

Use **Azure Cost Management** to track, analyze, and forecast spending.

Features:

- Per-resource and per-tag breakdowns
- Forecasting and trend analysis
- Budget creation with alert thresholds
- Cost anomaly detection

Example: Create a budget for App Service:

```
az consumption budget create \
  --amount 500 \
  --time-grain monthly \
  --budget-name dev-app-service \
  --category cost \
  --resource-group dev-rg
```

Performance and Cost Optimization Lifecycle

1. **Instrument**: Use Azure Monitor, App Insights, and diagnostic logs.

2. **Analyze**: Use KQL, Cost Analysis, and Advisor reports.

3. **Remediate**: Resize, re-tier, refactor, or re-architect.

4. **Automate**: Use DevOps, Bicep, or Terraform to enforce best practices.

5. **Iterate**: Continuous review and optimization based on telemetry.

Optimization Patterns

Pattern	Description
Burst Scaling	Use serverless or autoscale to handle unpredictable spikes
Lazy Loading	Load data only when needed to reduce storage and query overhead
Cold Storage Tiering	Offload archival data to cheaper storage tiers
Function Decomposition	Break monoliths into serverless components to optimize usage
Consolidated Monitoring	Aggregate logs and metrics to reduce workspace duplication and cost
Tag-Based Cost Allocation	Use tags (`env`, `owner`, `costCenter`) to track and limit spending

---

Best Practices

Area	Practice
Compute	Right-size, autoscale, use RIs/Spot where appropriate
Storage	Match tier to access pattern, automate lifecycle policies
Databases	Optimize queries, indexes, throughput, use elastic pools
Monitoring	Sample logs, set retention limits, filter categories
Budgets	Enforce cost limits by team, project, or environment
Automation	Bake optimization checks into pipelines using tools like Terraform Plan or `what-if`

| Reviews | Run cost and performance reviews quarterly |

Conclusion

Optimizing for performance and cost is a continuous journey, not a one-time activity. Azure provides a rich set of tools—Azure Monitor, Advisor, Cost Management, App Insights, and diagnostic logs—to empower teams to make informed decisions about infrastructure, services, and code.

By embedding observability, scaling patterns, and budgeting into the architecture and governance process, organizations can deliver high-performing applications that remain financially efficient and operationally robust—no matter how much they grow.

In the next section, we'll examine how DevOps practices and CI/CD pipelines can be scaled securely and reliably across environments, enabling faster releases without sacrificing control or compliance.

Scaling DevOps and CI/CD Pipelines

As organizations embrace cloud-native architecture and microservices, the velocity of software delivery becomes a critical competitive advantage. Azure supports modern DevOps practices that enable teams to ship code faster, more reliably, and with better governance. But to truly scale DevOps across multiple teams, environments, and business units, CI/CD pipelines must be designed as **shared, secure, repeatable, and observable systems**.

This section focuses on how to build, manage, and scale DevOps pipelines in Azure using tools such as Azure DevOps, GitHub Actions, Bicep, Terraform, and deployment strategies like blue-green, canary, and ring-based releases. It also covers best practices for secrets management, policy enforcement, and infrastructure as code (IaC).

The Goals of Scalable DevOps

- **Speed**: Accelerate time-to-market for new features.
- **Reliability**: Ensure consistent and repeatable deployments.
- **Security**: Protect code, credentials, and infrastructure throughout the pipeline.
- **Observability**: Trace every change, build, and deployment for auditing.
- **Governance**: Standardize pipelines across teams without stifling autonomy.

Scaling DevOps isn't just about tooling—it's about enabling **culture, process, and automation** to work together cohesively across the enterprise.

Core Components of CI/CD in Azure

Component	Purpose
Source Control	Git-based repositories (Azure Repos, GitHub)
Build Pipelines	Compile code, run tests, package artifacts
Release Pipelines	Deploy apps and infra to environments
IaC	Manage infrastructure declaratively
Secrets Management	Store keys and credentials securely
Observability	Monitor pipeline health, deployments, and changes
Policy & Guardrails	Enforce controls and approvals

Choosing a CI/CD Tool: Azure DevOps vs. GitHub Actions

Azure DevOps

- Mature enterprise-grade platform
- Boards, Repos, Pipelines, Artifacts, Test Plans
- YAML or classic UI pipelines
- Deep integration with Azure AD and approvals

GitHub Actions

- Git-native, integrated with pull requests
- Ideal for GitHub-hosted codebases

- Lightweight and flexible

- Growing support for enterprise features

Use Azure DevOps for larger organizations with complex release management. Use GitHub Actions for rapid developer workflows and open source collaboration.

Infrastructure as Code (IaC) at Scale

IaC allows you to define, version, and audit infrastructure alongside application code.

Supported tools:

- **Bicep**: Azure-native, declarative DSL for ARM templates

- **Terraform**: Cloud-agnostic, stateful, mature for multi-cloud use

- **Pulumi**: Uses general-purpose languages (TypeScript, Go, etc.)

- **ARM Templates**: JSON-based, less maintainable for large-scale use

Bicep Deployment Example

```
param location string = resourceGroup().location
param appName string

resource app 'Microsoft.Web/sites@2022-03-01' = {
  name: appName
  location: location
  kind: 'app'
  properties: {
    serverFarmId: 'myappserviceplan'
  }
}
```

Deploy using Azure CLI:

```
az deployment group create \
  --resource-group my-rg \
  --template-file main.bicep \
  --parameters appName=myapp
```

Use modules and parameter files for reusable components.

Secure CI/CD Pipelines

Security is paramount in automated deployments. Key practices include:

1. **Use managed identities** instead of service principals when possible.

2. Store secrets in **Azure Key Vault** and reference them at runtime.

3. Define **approval gates** and **environments** in release stages.

4. Audit every pipeline change and deployment via logging.

5. Integrate **static code analysis**, **dependency scanning**, and **container scanning**.

Example: Use Key Vault in GitHub Actions

```
- name: Azure Login
  uses: azure/login@v1
  with:
    creds: ${{ secrets.AZURE_CREDENTIALS }}

- name: Get secret
  uses: azure/get-keyvault-secrets@v1
  with:
    keyvault: 'my-keyvault'
    secrets: 'dbConnectionString'
```

Environments and Approvals

Define environments in your pipeline to reflect logical deployment stages:

- **Dev**: Fast iteration, minimal restrictions

- **Test/Staging**: Replica of prod, with data sanitization

- **Production**: Strict gating, monitored changes

Azure DevOps supports **multi-stage YAML pipelines** with approvals and checks:

```
stages:
  - stage: DeployToProd
    jobs:
      - deployment: Deploy
        environment: 'production'
        strategy:
          runOnce:
            deploy:
              steps:
                - script: echo 'Deploying to production'
```

Use **manual approvals**, **policy checks**, or **automated tests** as gates.

Deployment Strategies

1. Blue-Green Deployment

Deploy to a parallel environment ("green"), switch traffic when validated. Benefits:

- Fast   rollback

- Zero-downtime

- More   infrastructure   required

2. Canary Deployment

Gradually shift traffic to new version, monitor telemetry. Tools like **Azure Front Door**, **Traffic Manager**, or **App Gateway** can enable weighted routing.

3. Ring-Based Deployment

Release to a subset of users (e.g., internal, beta testers) before full production.

These strategies reduce risk and allow real-time feedback before global rollout.

Observability for DevOps

Build monitoring into your pipelines to track:

- Build   durations   and   failures

- Deployment success rate

- Time to recovery

- Change failure rate (DORA metrics)

Integrate with **Azure Monitor**, **Application Insights**, **Log Analytics**, and **Workbooks**.

Kusto query for deployment failures:

```
AzureDiagnostics
| where Category == "AzureDevOpsAudit"
| where ResultType == "Failed"
| summarize count() by bin(TimeGenerated, 1h), Caller
```

GitOps and Automation

GitOps is a model where **Git is the source of truth** for both code and infrastructure.

- Store desired state in Git

- Use pipelines or agents to reconcile actual state

- Enforce changes via pull requests and approvals

Tools like **Flux**, **ArgoCD**, and **Azure Arc-enabled Kubernetes** support GitOps for cluster management.

Scaling Across Teams

1. **Template Pipelines**: Create YAML templates for builds and releases.

2. **Reusable IaC Modules**: Standardize resource provisioning.

3. **Enforce Tags**: Tag resources for ownership, cost tracking.

4. **Policy as Code**: Enforce naming, tagging, location via Azure Policy.

5. **Landing Zones**: Use landing zones to give teams pre-configured environments.

Sample End-to-End CI/CD Flow

Tech Stack: GitHub → GitHub Actions → Bicep → Azure

1. Developer pushes code to `main`
2. GitHub Action triggers build, runs tests
3. If successful, triggers Bicep deployment to staging
4. Auto runs integration tests
5. Manual approval triggers production deployment
6. App Insights monitors post-release metrics
7. Alerts notify rollback triggers if needed

This model supports **speed, control, traceability**, and **recovery**.

Best Practices

Area	Practice
Secrets	Store in Azure Key Vault, never in repo or plain YAML
Environments	Use logical environments with approval gates
Templates	Create modular, parameterized pipeline templates
Deployment	Use canary/blue-green for sensitive workloads
Observability	Include deployment metrics and logging in every stage
Auditing	Track who deployed what, when, and why via commit metadata
Policy	Use Azure Policy to enforce IaC and pipeline configuration
Backup	Automate rollback pipelines and recovery points

Conclusion

Scaling DevOps and CI/CD pipelines in Azure requires thoughtful design, secure practices, and a strong automation culture. With the right tooling—Azure DevOps, GitHub Actions, Bicep, Terraform—and strategies like GitOps and environment gating, organizations can deliver applications faster and with greater confidence.

A scalable DevOps model not only increases release velocity but also enhances stability, compliance, and team autonomy. In the next chapter, we'll explore architectural patterns for hyper-scale applications, including microservices, serverless workloads, and event-driven design in Azure.

Chapter 9: Advanced Patterns for Hyper-Scale Applications

Microservices and Event-Driven Architecture in Azure

Building for hyper-scale demands more than horizontal scaling and auto-provisioning—it requires an architectural paradigm shift. Traditional monolithic applications, while easier to develop initially, become bottlenecks in systems that require agility, elasticity, and resilience. **Microservices architecture** combined with **event-driven patterns** forms the backbone of scalable, distributed systems in the cloud.

Azure offers a wide range of services that enable microservices and event-driven architectures, such as Azure Kubernetes Service (AKS), Azure Service Bus, Azure Event Grid, Azure Functions, and Azure Container Apps. This section explores how to architect, deploy, and manage microservices-based systems on Azure and how to decouple workloads using events to enhance performance, maintainability, and fault tolerance.

What Are Microservices?

Microservices are an architectural style that structures an application as a collection of **loosely coupled**, **independently deployable** services, each of which implements a specific business capability.

Core Characteristics

- **Single Responsibility**: Each microservice does one thing well.

- **Independence**: Services can be deployed, scaled, and updated independently.

- **Decentralization**: Teams own their services end-to-end, including storage and release pipelines.

- **Technology Diversity**: Services can be written in different languages or use different data stores.

- **Resilience**: Failures are isolated and do not affect the entire system.

Azure's native tooling and services are designed to support this model at scale.

Azure Services for Microservices

Service	Purpose
Azure Kubernetes Service (AKS)	Orchestrate and scale containerized workloads
Azure Container Apps	Run microservices with built-in autoscaling and Dapr
Azure Functions	Execute business logic in response to events
Azure App Service	Host individual services in isolated environments
Azure API Management	Provide a unified API gateway
Azure Key Vault	Secure service secrets and credentials
Azure DevOps / GitHub	Automate CI/CD pipelines for independent services

Microservices Deployment Strategies

1. Azure Kubernetes Service (AKS)

AKS is a managed Kubernetes platform for orchestrating containers and microservices.

- Use Helm charts or Kustomize for deployments.
- Integrate Azure Monitor for observability.
- Implement network policies and Azure CNI for secure communication.
- Enable Horizontal Pod Autoscaler (HPA) and Cluster Autoscaler.

Example HPA configuration:

```
apiVersion: autoscaling/v2
kind: HorizontalPodAutoscaler
metadata:
  name: orderservice-hpa
spec:
  scaleTargetRef:
    apiVersion: apps/v1
    kind: Deployment
```

```
  name: orderservice
minReplicas: 2
maxReplicas: 10
metrics:
  - type: Resource
    resource:
      name: cpu
      target:
        type: Utilization
        averageUtilization: 70
```

2. Azure Container Apps

Container Apps simplify microservices deployment with built-in autoscaling, revisions, and traffic splitting.

Benefits:

- Serverless scaling down to zero
- Dapr integration for service discovery and state management
- HTTP and event-driven ingress support
- Pay-per-use pricing

Use cases: APIs, background workers, real-time processing.

API Gateway Pattern with Azure API Management

Microservices expose APIs, but direct client access to each service increases complexity and security risks. The **API Gateway pattern** solves this by providing a single entry point.

Azure API Management (APIM) enables:

- Centralized API documentation
- Rate limiting and throttling
- JWT validation and OAuth2 support
- Header and query string rewriting

- Internal vs. external routing

Example APIM policy to enforce subscription key:

```
<inbound>
  <base />
  <check-header name="Ocp-Apim-Subscription-Key" failed-check-
httpcode="401" />
</inbound>
```

Event-Driven Architecture (EDA)

EDA decouples producers and consumers via events, increasing system agility and scalability. Instead of synchronous HTTP calls, services communicate via **event streams**, **queues**, or **pub-sub** models.

Benefits of EDA

- Loose coupling

- Horizontal scalability

- Fault isolation

- Asynchronous processing

- Real-time data flow

Azure Eventing Services

Service	Description	Use Case
Azure Event Grid	Event routing with publish/subscribe semantics	Serverless triggers, system events
Azure Service Bus	Message broker with queues and topics	Order processing, payment handling
Azure Event Hubs	High-throughput event ingestion pipeline	Telemetry, analytics, logging

Azure Queue	Storage	Simple message queue within storage accounts	Lightweight decoupling

Using Event Grid with Azure Functions

Example: Event-driven image processing with Azure Storage and Functions

1. Blob uploaded to Storage container

2. Event Grid triggers Azure Function

3. Function performs image resizing

4. Result stored in another container

Function template:

```csharp
public static class ImageResizer
{
    [FunctionName("ImageResizer")]
    public static void Run(
        [EventGridTrigger] EventGridEvent eventGridEvent,
        ILogger log)
    {
        // Deserialize event and process blob
    }
}
```

Choreography vs. Orchestration

- **Choreography**: Each service reacts to events independently.
    - Pros: Decoupled, scalable
    - Cons: Harder to visualize flow
- **Orchestration**: A central coordinator (e.g., Durable Function, Logic App) manages workflow.
    - Pros: Easier to model business processes

- ○ Cons: Introduces   central   dependency

Azure Durable Functions provide orchestration with stateful workflows, retries, and timers.

State Management in Microservices

State is a key challenge in distributed systems.

Options:

- **Stateless services**: Use databases, caches, or queues for state.

- **Stateful services**: Use Azure SQL, Cosmos DB, or Azure Cache for Redis.

- **Dapr state store**: Abstracted, pluggable state backend for Container Apps.

Avoid direct data coupling between services. Use **event sourcing** or **data replication** patterns to maintain autonomy.

Observability in Distributed Architectures

Key pillars:

- **Tracing**: Use OpenTelemetry with Azure Monitor for end-to-end visibility.

- **Logging**: Centralize logs in Log Analytics or Azure Data Explorer.

- **Metrics**: Use Prometheus, Azure Monitor, and Grafana.

- **Correlation IDs**: Propagate IDs across requests and events.

Enable Application Insights and set up custom telemetry with distributed trace correlation.

Resilience and Fault Tolerance

Strategies:

- **Retries**   **with**   **exponential**   **backoff**

- **Circuit breakers** (e.g., Polly in .NET)

- **Timeouts** and **bulkheads**

- **Dead-letter queues** for failed messages

Azure Service Bus and Event Grid support dead-lettering out of the box.

Example: Enable DLQ in Service Bus subscription

```
az servicebus topic subscription create \
  --resource-group my-rg \
  --namespace-name mynamespace \
  --topic-name orders \
  --name orders-subscription \
  --enable-dead-lettering-on-message-expiration true
```

Organizational Considerations

- Organize teams around **business capabilities**, not technology layers.

- Use **bounded contexts** and **domain-driven design** (DDD).

- Empower teams with **end-to-end ownership** (build, run, monitor).

- Standardize deployment pipelines but allow service autonomy.

Best Practices

Area	Best Practice
Deployment	Use AKS or Container Apps with autoscaling
Communication	Prefer async messaging over synchronous calls
APIs	Use API Management as the gateway with caching and throttling
Eventing	Use Event Grid for integration, Service Bus for transactions

Observability	Implement distributed tracing and central logging
CI/CD	Deploy services independently using GitHub Actions or Azure DevOps
Security	Secure services with managed identities, Key Vault, and NSGs

Conclusion

Microservices and event-driven architecture are the building blocks of modern, hyper-scalable systems. Azure provides robust and scalable platforms—like AKS, Container Apps, Event Grid, and Service Bus—to support this architecture at scale. By designing for autonomy, observability, and resilience, teams can build modular systems that evolve rapidly and perform reliably under any load.

In the next section, we will dive into serverless computing with Azure Functions and Durable Entities, exploring how to scale logic execution elastically without managing infrastructure.

Serverless Scaling with Azure Functions and Durable Entities

In the evolving landscape of cloud-native development, serverless computing has emerged as a powerful model for building scalable and event-driven applications with minimal operational overhead. Azure Functions, Microsoft's serverless compute offering, enables developers to run small pieces of code (functions) in the cloud without worrying about infrastructure provisioning, maintenance, or scaling. When combined with **Durable Functions** and **Durable Entities**, this model allows for orchestrating complex workflows and maintaining reliable, stateful interactions across distributed systems.

This section explores how to architect solutions using Azure Functions and Durable Entities to achieve elastic scalability, improve efficiency, reduce operational burden, and embrace modern application patterns like microservices, data pipelines, real-time processing, and long-running orchestrations.

The Serverless Paradigm

Serverless computing abstracts the infrastructure layer, allowing developers to focus purely on code. With serverless:

- You don't manage servers.
- Billing is based on execution time and invocations.

- Scaling is automatic—down to zero or up to thousands of instances.

- Services are event-driven by design.

Azure Functions epitomize this by allowing small units of logic to run in response to triggers such as HTTP requests, queue messages, database updates, and timers.

Azure Functions: Core Concepts

Triggers and Bindings

Azure Functions are powered by **triggers** and **bindings**:

- **Trigger**: Defines how a function is invoked (e.g., HTTP, Timer, Event Hub).

- **Input binding**: Passes data into a function.

- **Output binding**: Sends data from a function to another service.

Example: HTTP-triggered function with Blob Storage output

```
[FunctionName("UploadFile")]
public static async Task<IActionResult> Run(
    [HttpTrigger(AuthorizationLevel.Function, "post", Route = null)]
HttpRequest req,
    [Blob("uploads/{rand-guid}.txt", FileAccess.Write, Connection =
"StorageConnectionAppSetting")] Stream outputBlob,
    ILogger log)
{
    await req.Body.CopyToAsync(outputBlob);
    return new OkObjectResult("File uploaded.");
}
```

Hosting and Plans

Azure Functions can run in multiple plans:

Plan	Description

Consumption	Auto-scales, pay-per-execution, ideal for burst workloads
Premium	Scales faster with VNET support and unlimited execution time
Dedicated (App Service Plan)	For long-running, predictable workloads with existing App Service infra

Use **Premium Plan** for production-scale workloads requiring low cold-start latency and advanced networking features.

Durable Functions

Durable Functions extend Azure Functions by adding support for **stateful workflows** and **long-running operations** using the **Async/Await** programming model.

Key components:

- **Orchestrator Function**: Coordinates the workflow.
- **Activity Function**: Executes discrete units of work.
- **Client Function**: Starts the orchestration.

Benefits

- Durable and replayable workflows
- Simplified coding model for fan-out/fan-in patterns
- Built-in support for retries, timeouts, and checkpoints
- Scales automatically with load

Durable Function Example: Fan-out/Fan-in Pattern

```
[FunctionName("OrchestratorFunction")]
public static async Task<List<string>> RunOrchestrator(
    [OrchestrationTrigger] IDurableOrchestrationContext context)
{
    var outputs = new List<string>();
```

```
    var tasks = new List<Task<string>>();

    for (int i = 0; i < 5; i++)
    {
        tasks.Add(context.CallActivityAsync<string>("ProcessItem",
i));
    }

    await Task.WhenAll(tasks);

    foreach (var result in tasks)
    {
        outputs.Add(result.Result);
    }

    return outputs;
}

[FunctionName("ProcessItem")]
public static string ProcessItem([ActivityTrigger] int item, ILogger
log)
{
    return $"Processed item {item}";
}
```

This architecture is resilient to failure and automatically replays incomplete work when restarted.

Durable Entities

Durable Entities offer a **lightweight actor model** for managing stateful objects with Azure Functions.

Features

- Entity functions encapsulate both state and behavior.

- Scales horizontally across regions and partitions.

- Ideal for counters, registries, shopping carts, IoT devices.

Example: Entity Function to Track Inventory

```csharp
[JsonObject(MemberSerialization.OptIn)]
public class Inventory
{
    [JsonProperty("count")]
    public int Count { get; set; }

    [FunctionName(nameof(Inventory))]
    public static Task Run([EntityTrigger] IDurableEntityContext ctx)
        => ctx.DispatchAsync<Inventory>();

    public void Add(int value) => Count += value;
    public void Remove(int value) => Count -= value;
    public int Get() => Count;
}
```

Invoke entity functions from orchestrations or directly via REST or client SDKs.

Event-Driven Patterns with Azure Functions

Azure Functions naturally support **event-driven architecture**, integrating seamlessly with:

- **Azure** **Event** **Grid**

- **Azure** **Service** **Bus**

- **Azure** **Event** **Hubs**

- **Storage** **Queues**

This enables powerful use cases such as:

- Processing files as soon as they're uploaded

- Reacting to user signups or purchases

- Executing background jobs on demand

- Coordinating order fulfillment pipelines

Integration with Dapr

For advanced microservice patterns, Azure Container Apps and Azure Functions support **Dapr**:

- Sidecar model for service discovery, state management, and pub/sub

- Use bindings to external systems like Redis, Kafka, and PostgreSQL

- Simplifies event handling across services

Dapr + Azure Functions = fast, portable event-driven logic with no boilerplate code for common patterns.

Observability and Reliability

Monitor and trace Azure Functions with:

- **Application Insights**: Automatically collects traces, metrics, dependencies

- **Log Analytics**: Query logs with Kusto (KQL)

- **Azure Monitor Alerts**: Trigger on failures, exceptions, or latency

Enable durable function history tracking:

```
DurableFunctionsEvents
| where FunctionName == "OrchestratorFunction"
| summarize count() by EventTypeName, bin(Timestamp, 5m)
```

Scaling Characteristics

Feature	Consumption Plan	Premium Plan
Cold Starts	Yes (some delay)	No
VNET Integration	No	Yes
Scaling Speed	Moderate	Fast

Max Execution Time	5–10 mins	Unlimited
Cost Model	Per-execution	Per-instance

Use **Premium Plan or Container Apps** for enterprise scenarios requiring VNET, predictable latency, or large state.

Security Best Practices

- Use **managed identities** to access Azure resources securely.
- Store secrets in **Azure Key Vault**, not in environment variables.
- Use **API Management** or **Azure Front Door** to expose and secure function endpoints.
- Apply **RBAC** and **App Service authentication** for access control.

Example: Secure a function with Azure AD

```
"authLevel": "function",
"identity": {
  "type": "SystemAssigned"
}
```

CI/CD for Serverless

Deploy functions via:

- **Azure DevOps pipelines**
- **GitHub Actions**
- **ARM/Bicep/Terraform templates**
- **Azure CLI / PowerShell**

Example GitHub Action for deployment:

```
- uses: azure/functions-action@v1
  with:
```

```
app-name: 'my-function-app'
package: '.'
```

Automate infrastructure and application deployment together for consistent rollouts.

Best Practices

Area	Recommendation
Design	Keep functions small and single-purpose
State	Use Durable Entities or external stores like Cosmos DB
Deployment	Use slots for safe deployment and rollback
Scaling	Choose Premium Plan for low latency and network isolation
Events	Use Event Grid + Durable Functions for complex orchestration
Resilience	Implement retries, error handling, and DLQs
Monitoring	Enable Application Insights and set alerts on failure/latency
Secrets	Use Key Vault and managed identities

Conclusion

Azure Functions and Durable Entities enable developers to build powerful, scalable, and cost-efficient solutions without managing infrastructure. Whether you're handling millions of events, coordinating distributed workflows, or maintaining fine-grained state in a cloud-native system, serverless architecture delivers the agility and scale modern applications demand.

By combining serverless compute with event-driven design, you can build hyper-scale systems that react instantly to change, scale with demand, and recover from failures gracefully—all while minimizing complexity and cost. In the next section, we will explore how to apply Microsoft's Well-Architected Framework to design robust, scalable, and operationally excellent cloud solutions.

Designing with the Well-Architected Framework

The Azure Well-Architected Framework (WAF) is a collection of guiding principles, best practices, and design tenets developed by Microsoft to help architects build secure, scalable, and resilient cloud applications. As organizations grow and operate at scale, these principles become increasingly critical for sustaining performance, minimizing risk, and optimizing costs across distributed systems.

This section provides an in-depth look at how to design enterprise-grade architectures using the five pillars of the Well-Architected Framework: **Cost Optimization**, **Operational Excellence**, **Performance Efficiency**, **Reliability**, and **Security**. By applying these principles systematically, architects can align technical decisions with business goals, improve system maturity, and accelerate innovation without compromising control.

Overview of the Five Pillars

Pillar	Focus Area
Cost Optimization	Managing costs while delivering business value
Operational Excellence	Monitoring, automation, and continuous improvement
Performance Efficiency	Efficient use of computing resources to meet requirements
Reliability	Ensuring systems can recover from failures and meet availability targets
Security	Protecting applications and data from threats

The Well-Architected Framework provides a **structured review process** for evaluating architecture quality and identifying areas for improvement.

1. Cost Optimization

Cost optimization in cloud architecture involves delivering business value at the lowest price point. Azure provides native tools to monitor, forecast, and control spending.

Key Design Principles

- Adopt a **pay-as-you-go** model

- Monitor and allocate spend by workload
- Optimize resource utilization (right-size)
- Use managed services where possible
- Apply tagging for cost visibility

Best Practices

- Use **Azure Cost Management** and **Budgets** to track spending.
- Implement **auto-scaling** to avoid over-provisioning.
- Replace monolithic VMs with **containerized microservices**.
- Use **spot VMs** for interruptible workloads.
- Consider **Azure Reservations** for long-term usage (VMs, SQL, Cosmos DB).

```
az consumption budget create \
  --resource-group billing-rg \
  --budget-name dev-budget \
  --amount 500 \
  --time-grain Monthly \
  --category Cost \
  --start-date 2025-01-01 \
  --end-date 2025-12-31
```

---

2. Operational Excellence

Operational excellence focuses on operations processes that keep systems running in production reliably and efficiently. This pillar emphasizes monitoring, automation, incident response, and continuous improvement.

Key Design Principles

- Enable **observability** by **default**
- Automate routine operations
- Validate changes before deployment

- Use infrastructure as code (IaC)
- Conduct regular post-incident reviews

Best Practices

- Deploy monitoring with **Azure Monitor** and **Log Analytics**.
- Use **App Insights** to track application health and user behavior.
- Define alert rules and **action groups** for proactive remediation.
- Integrate CI/CD with **GitHub Actions** or **Azure DevOps**.
- Use **Azure Automation** or **Logic Apps** for routine tasks (e.g., patching, backups).

```
- uses: azure/arm-deploy@v1
  with:
    resourceGroupName: 'prod-rg'
    template: './main.bicep'
    parameters: environment=prod
```

---

3. Performance Efficiency

This pillar addresses how efficiently systems use resources and how they adapt to changing requirements. It ensures systems deliver consistent performance under varying load conditions.

Key Design Principles

- Match resource types and sizes to workloads
- Use caching to reduce latency
- Measure and adapt continuously
- Leverage scalable managed services

Best Practices

- Use **Azure Front Door** or **CDN** to reduce latency for global users.

- Cache frequent data with **Azure Cache for Redis**.
- Use **autoscaling** for App Services, VMSS, or Container Apps.
- Choose the right compute tier: serverless, premium, or dedicated.
- Apply **load testing** before scaling out.

Example: Enable autoscale for App Service Plan

```
az monitor autoscale create \
  --resource
/subscriptions/{id}/resourceGroups/{rg}/providers/Microsoft.Web/serv
erfarms/myAppServicePlan \
  --min-count 2 \
  --max-count 10 \
  --count 2
```

---

4. Reliability

Reliability ensures that workloads can recover from disruptions and meet their availability and continuity targets. It encompasses both **resilient design** and **operational recovery**.

Key Design Principles

- Design for **high availability** and **disaster recovery**
- Use **redundant components**
- Apply retry logic and circuit breakers
- Plan for **failure** **at** **every** **level**

Best Practices

- Use **Availability Zones** and **Availability Sets** for fault tolerance.
- Deploy **active-active** or **active-passive** architecture across regions.
- Use **geo-redundant storage** for backup data.
- Implement **auto-failover** for databases (e.g., Azure SQL, Cosmos DB).

- Monitor SLAs and implement synthetic checks.

Durable Functions and Retry policies help gracefully handle transient errors in serverless apps.

---

5. Security

Security protects applications, data, and infrastructure from threats. It spans identity, data protection, network controls, and monitoring.

Key Design Principles

- Apply **Zero Trust**: verify explicitly, use least privilege
- Centralize identity with **Azure AD**
- Protect secrets with **Key Vault**
- Enable **network segmentation**
- Encrypt data in transit and at rest

Best Practices

- Use **managed identities** for secure authentication to Azure services.
- Apply **Azure RBAC** and **PIM** (Privileged Identity Management).
- Monitor threats with **Microsoft Defender for Cloud**.
- Enforce policy with **Azure Policy** and **BluePrints**.
- Use **WAF**, NSGs, and firewalls for network protection.

Example: Assign role using RBAC

```
az role assignment create \
  --assignee user@example.com \
  --role "Contributor" \
  --scope "/subscriptions/{id}/resourceGroups/my-rg"
```

Azure Well-Architected Review Tool

Microsoft provides the **Well-Architected Review (WAR)** tool for assessing workloads against the five pillars. It produces a report with recommendations and prioritized actions.

Tool location: https://aka.ms/azwar

Use it periodically to:

- Assess workloads as they evolve
- Evaluate new architectures
- Justify technical decisions
- Align solutions with business priorities

Integrating WAF into the Development Lifecycle

1. **Design Phase**: Use WAF to evaluate architectural decisions.
2. **Build Phase**: Implement telemetry, security, and IaC from the beginning.
3. **Deploy Phase**: Automate checks and approvals via CI/CD.
4. **Operate Phase**: Continuously monitor cost, performance, and resilience.
5. **Iterate**: Treat architecture as a living artifact—refactor, review, and optimize.

Embed WAF checklists and gates in your release pipelines. For example, block production releases if SLA, budget, or policy thresholds are exceeded.

Organizational Alignment

- Assign **pillar champions** in teams to own WAF categories.
- Run **quarterly WAR assessments** for key applications.
- Include WAF metrics in executive dashboards.
- Use WAF reviews as part of **go-live** checklists.

- Educate developers and architects with Microsoft Learn and certification paths (e.g., AZ-305).

Best Practices Summary

Pillar	Key Practices
Cost Optimization	Use reservations, autoscale, shut down idle resources
Operational Excellence	Automate, monitor, log, and postmortem
Performance	Tune caching, scale efficiently, use CDN/Edge
Reliability	Use zones, replication, retries, and backup
Security	Enforce identity, use encryption, audit, and secure endpoints

---

Conclusion

The Azure Well-Architected Framework is not a one-time exercise but a continuous commitment to excellence. It ensures that every workload deployed to the cloud is aligned with business outcomes, designed for resilience, secured by default, cost-aware, and ready to scale.

By embedding these pillars into your architecture reviews, development pipelines, and operational procedures, you not only create better systems—you build confidence that those systems will perform, scale, and recover no matter the demand. In the next chapter, we'll turn theory into practice by examining real-world implementations and case studies across industries like finance, retail, and the public sector.

Chapter 10: Case Studies and Real-World Implementations

Enterprise Scale Deployment for Financial Services

The financial services sector is a prime candidate for adopting scalable cloud architecture due to its demand for high availability, low latency, secure processing, and regulatory compliance. Institutions ranging from global banks to fintech startups are leveraging Azure to modernize their platforms, improve customer experience, and reduce operational risk. This section presents a detailed case study of an enterprise-scale Azure deployment in the financial industry, showcasing architectural decisions, regulatory considerations, security enforcement, and operational best practices.

Background and Objectives

A multinational banking institution—referred to here as "FinTrust Bank"—faced growing pressure to digitize its legacy core banking platform. The goals of the initiative included:

- Migrating on-premises workloads to Azure for elasticity and cost efficiency.

- Creating a scalable, modular platform to support new products and channels.

- Enhancing security posture and aligning with PCI DSS, GDPR, and regional regulations.

- Reducing time-to-market for new features via DevOps and microservices adoption.

- Ensuring business continuity with multi-region disaster recovery.

Architecture Overview

The solution was built on the following architectural pillars:

- **Azure Kubernetes Service (AKS)** for microservices orchestration.

- **Azure API Management (APIM)** as a secure API gateway.

- **Azure Key Vault** for centralized secret and certificate management.

- **Azure SQL Database Hyperscale** and **Cosmos DB** for data storage.

- **Azure Event Grid** and **Service Bus** for messaging and event-driven processing.

- **Azure Front Door** and **Traffic Manager** for global request routing.

- **Azure Policy, Blueprints,** and **Management Groups** for governance.

A multi-region deployment model with **active-active failover** was established to support mission-critical services across the U.S. and Europe.

Identity and Access Management

To ensure strict access control and support for multi-national staff and external vendors:

- **Azure Active Directory (AAD)** with Conditional Access was implemented.

- **Privileged Identity Management (PIM)** enforced just-in-time (JIT) elevation.

- Role-Based Access Control (RBAC) was defined at resource group and subscription levels.

- Admin and developer groups were assigned minimal permissions using AAD groups.

Sensitive workloads were further isolated using **network segmentation** and **private endpoints**.

Data Strategy and Compliance

The solution required handling sensitive Personally Identifiable Information (PII), credit card data, and transaction records.

Data Storage Design

Requirement	Implementation
Structured financial records	Azure SQL Hyperscale with geo-replication
Semi-structured event logs	Azure Cosmos DB with partitioned containers

Historical reporting	Azure Data Lake Gen2 with long-term retention
Real-time analytics	Azure Synapse Analytics and Power BI

Compliance Considerations

- Data encryption at rest using **customer-managed keys (CMK)**.

- Transport Layer Security (TLS 1.2+) enforced for all services.

- Integration with **Azure Purview** for data lineage and classification.

- **Activity logging** and **log retention** implemented via Log Analytics.

Regular audits and penetration tests were scheduled through Azure Security Center recommendations.

Application Design and Resiliency

The core application was refactored into over 30 microservices, grouped into bounded contexts:

- **Accounts**

- **Payments**

- **Risk** and **Compliance**

- **Customer** **Engagement**

- **Reporting** and **Analytics**

Resiliency Features

- **Retries and exponential backoff** in client and service communication.

- **Dead-letter queues (DLQs)** for Service Bus topics.

- Durable Functions for **long-running orchestrations** like account reconciliation.

- **Geo-redundancy** for databases and storage accounts.

- **Traffic splitting** and **gradual rollout** using Azure Front Door routing rules.

Each service was independently deployable via its own CI/CD pipeline using Azure DevOps.

DevOps and CI/CD Implementation

To enable continuous delivery with governance:

- **Infrastructure as Code (IaC)**: All Azure resources provisioned with Bicep and Terraform.

- **Multi-stage YAML pipelines**: Environments configured for dev, QA, UAT, and prod.

- **Approvals and gates**: Required for production release stages.

- **Artifact promotion**: Used Azure Artifacts to control version progression.

Example pipeline stage configuration:

```
stages:
- stage: DeployToProd
  jobs:
    - deployment: ProdDeploy
      environment: 'Production'
      strategy:
        runOnce:
          deploy:
            steps:
              - task: AzureCLI@2
                inputs:
                  scriptType: bash
```

```
        scriptLocation: inlineScript

        inlineScript: |

          az deployment group create \

            --template-file main.bicep \

            --resource-group fintrust-prod
```

Secrets and credentials were managed using Key Vault references in pipeline variables.

Monitoring and Observability

Enterprise observability was built using Azure-native tools:

- **Azure Monitor** and **Log Analytics** for infrastructure health and performance.

- **Application Insights** for end-to-end tracing of customer interactions.

- **Custom dashboards** for SLA monitoring, regional health, and usage trends.

- **Workbooks** for security posture, API usage, and service KPIs.

- **Alerts** routed to DevSecOps via Teams, PagerDuty, and ITSM systems.

Example KQL query for failed payment transactions:

```
requests

| where cloud_RoleName == "payment-service"

| where success == false

| summarize count() by bin(timestamp, 5m), resultCode
```

Security Hardening

Security was embedded in every layer:

- **Network security groups (NSGs)** and **firewalls** at subnet and resource level.
- **Private endpoints** for all PaaS services.
- **Web Application Firewall (WAF)** with Azure Front Door.
- **Azure Defender for Cloud** enabled across subscriptions.
- **Security Center recommendations** reviewed weekly and automated via playbooks.

Business Outcomes

After a 9-month phased migration and optimization cycle, FinTrust Bank reported:

- 47% reduction in operational infrastructure costs
- 99.99% uptime across all banking services
- New product rollout times reduced from 3 months to 3 weeks
- Full PCI-DSS and GDPR compliance achieved in Azure
- 60% improvement in developer release velocity

Lessons Learned

1. **Start with governance**: Implement management groups, policies, and naming standards before deployment.

2. **Design for compliance**: Regulatory alignment should guide data architecture and access control.

3. **Automate everything**: CI/CD, IaC, security remediation, and reporting should be automated.

4. **Observe everything**: Telemetry must cover both user activity and service health.

5. **Don't lift-and-shift**: Refactor workloads to leverage platform-native features.

Conclusion

Enterprise-scale cloud transformation in the financial services sector is both complex and rewarding. Azure's platform provides the building blocks—when paired with architectural discipline, automation, and governance—that enable secure, scalable, and resilient financial applications. The FinTrust Bank case study demonstrates how modernization can be achieved without compromising security or compliance, and how DevOps and microservices accelerate innovation while meeting strict SLAs.

In the next section, we will explore a global e-commerce platform that scaled to handle millions of transactions per day using Azure-native services and cloud-native design principles.

Global E-Commerce Platform Scalability

E-commerce is a sector where scalability, reliability, and performance are not just desirable—they are non-negotiable. A global e-commerce platform must support thousands of concurrent users, high transaction volumes, fluctuating traffic patterns during seasonal peaks, and complex integrations with third-party systems. This case study explores the architectural approach of "ShopGlobal" (a fictionalized representation based on real-world implementations) in building a high-performance, globally distributed e-commerce platform on Microsoft Azure.

The case focuses on how Azure services were used to meet business goals, the challenges encountered in operating at scale, and the design decisions that enabled growth, resilience, and agility.

Project Goals and Requirements

ShopGlobal aimed to redesign their legacy commerce platform to:

- Support a global user base with <200ms latency.

- Achieve 99.99% uptime with geo-redundancy.

- Scale elastically to accommodate peak events (e.g., Black Friday).

- Handle over 500,000 concurrent sessions and 100,000 orders per minute.

- Ensure security and compliance with GDPR and PCI-DSS.

- Accelerate product launch and content updates.

High-Level Architecture Overview

The new platform was designed using a cloud-native, modular architecture with the following core components:

- **Azure Kubernetes Service (AKS)**: Orchestrating containerized microservices.

- **Azure Cosmos DB**: Globally distributed, multi-model database.

- **Azure Front Door**: Global load balancing and edge acceleration.

- **Azure Functions**: Serverless processing for background jobs.

- **Azure API Management (APIM)**: API gateway for customer and partner APIs.

- **Azure Blob Storage and CDN**: Media storage and delivery for product images and assets.

- **Azure Event Grid and Service Bus**: Asynchronous messaging backbone.

- **Azure DevOps and GitHub Actions**: CI/CD automation.

Each service was deployed in a **multi-region active-active** configuration with failover via Azure Traffic Manager.

Core Services Breakdown

1. Product Catalog Microservice

- Hosted on AKS, with read replicas in each region.

- Backed by Cosmos DB using partitioning based on product category.

- Cached frequently accessed items using Azure Redis Cache.

2. Shopping Cart and Session Handling

- Session state stored in Redis to ensure low-latency reads.

- Shopping cart service used Durable Entities to persist cart state with eventual consistency.

- Implemented automatic cart recovery and inactivity timeout workflows.

3. Checkout and Payment

- PCI-compliant payment orchestration built using Azure Functions and Logic Apps.

- Payments routed to third-party gateways via APIM with retries and fallback.

```
[FunctionName("ProcessPayment")]

public async Task<IActionResult> Run(

    [HttpTrigger(AuthorizationLevel.Function, "post")] HttpRequest
req,

    ILogger log)

{

    // Deserialize request and call payment gateway API

    return new OkObjectResult("Payment processed");

}
```

4. Order Fulfillment and Logistics

- Events published to Event Grid on successful order placement.
- Order service subscribers trigger fulfillment workflows via Durable Functions.
- Third-party logistics APIs integrated via Logic Apps with retry policies and throttling.

Data Strategy

Cosmos DB

- Used **multi-region write** mode to support low-latency read/write.
- Partitioned order documents by customer ID.
- TTL settings configured for temporary documents (e.g., session tokens).

```
{

    "id": "order-45782",
```

```
"customerId": "1234",

"status": "confirmed",

"items": [...],

"region": "eastus"
}
```

Azure SQL Database

- Used for transactional reporting and batch exports.
- Synapse pipelines pulled data nightly into Data Lake Gen2 for analytics.

Search

- Azure Cognitive Search indexed product catalogs with AI-powered image and text enrichment.
- Faceted navigation enabled category filtering and type-ahead search.

Scalability Measures

Horizontal Scaling

- All microservices deployed with HPA on AKS.
- Redis autoscaled based on memory and CPU thresholds.
- Cosmos DB RUs adjusted dynamically using Azure CLI scripts during peak periods.

```
az cosmosdb sql container throughput update \

  --account-name shopglobal-db \

  --database-name catalog \

  --name products \

  --throughput 100000
```

Global Distribution

- Front Door terminated SSL at edge POPs and routed traffic to nearest region.

- Product images delivered via Azure CDN with rules for dynamic vs. static content.

- Cosmos DB and App Services deployed in East US, West Europe, Southeast Asia.

Rate Limiting and Throttling

- Azure API Management policies enforced per-user and per-IP request limits.

- Custom 429 responses guided clients to retry or queue low-priority requests.

DevOps and Release Engineering

- All environments (dev, QA, staging, prod) built from the same infrastructure codebase using   Bicep.

- GitHub Actions used for app builds; Azure DevOps pipelines for infrastructure and deployment.

```
jobs:
  - job: Deploy
    steps:
      - uses: azure/cli@v1
        with:
          inlineScript: |
            az deployment group create \
              --resource-group shop-prod \
              --template-file main.bicep
```

- Canary releases implemented via Front Door rules and feature flags.
- Revisions in Container Apps enabled zero-downtime deployments with rollback support.

Monitoring and Observability

- Azure Monitor tracked system-level metrics across Kubernetes clusters.
- App Insights instrumented all APIs and services with correlation IDs.
- Alerts created for latency, error rates, SKU availability, and payment failures.
- Workbooks displayed live dashboards with heatmaps by region and device.

Sample KQL query to monitor payment failures:

```
requests
| where cloud_RoleName == "payment-service"
| where success == false
| summarize count() by resultCode, bin(timestamp, 5m)
```

- Diagnostic settings shipped all logs to centralized Log Analytics workspace with 180-day retention.

Resilience and Failover

- Active-active deployment ensured regional isolation of failures.
- AKS clusters used **pod disruption budgets** and **node affinity** to control placement and availability.
- Cosmos DB auto-failover tested quarterly across write regions.
- Traffic Manager enabled region failover with health probes.

Security and Compliance

- Azure AD B2C handled customer authentication with MFA and social login.
- Managed identities secured access to storage, databases, and queues.
- API access controlled via OAuth 2.0 and APIM key validation policies.
- Penetration testing conducted quarterly; WAF policies updated automatically via DevSecOps pipeline.

Business Outcomes

- Order throughput increased by 10x with no impact on latency.
- Platform supported 3.5 million users during Black Friday with 99.999% availability.
- Developer productivity doubled with reduced deployment friction.
- Multi-region resilience led to <3 minute RTO and near-zero RPO.
- Average page load time reduced to <1s globally due to CDN and Front Door optimization.

Lessons Learned

- **Data partitioning is key**: Improperly partitioned Cosmos DB containers were the root of several early scalability issues.
- **Global testing matters**: Load balancing configurations need regional traffic simulation, not just simulated load.
- **Observability fuels agility**: Without full-stack telemetry, rollout confidence is significantly lower.
- **Decouple with events**: Asynchronous processing was the cornerstone of system resilience.

- **Feature flags are invaluable**: Helped progressively release and validate features under real load.

Conclusion

The ShopGlobal case study illustrates the power of Azure's native services and architectural best practices in delivering a highly scalable, resilient, and performant e-commerce platform. By leveraging microservices, serverless workflows, global distribution, and DevOps automation, the organization was able to meet peak demand, innovate rapidly, and deliver world-class digital experiences to millions of users worldwide.

In the next section, we'll explore how public sector and government entities are harnessing Azure to deliver scalable and compliant digital services across healthcare, justice, education, and more.

Public Sector and Government Cloud Use Cases

Governments and public sector organizations face unique challenges in their digital transformation journeys: stringent security and compliance requirements, legacy infrastructure constraints, data sovereignty regulations, and the need for high availability of mission-critical services. At the same time, they are under pressure to improve citizen engagement, deliver services at scale, reduce costs, and enhance operational agility.

Azure's comprehensive platform and compliance-ready environment make it an ideal choice for public institutions seeking modernization without compromising on control or governance. This section examines how various public sector organizations—across healthcare, justice, education, and civic administration—have leveraged Azure to create secure, scalable, and efficient digital services.

Government Cloud Adoption Drivers

- **Security & Compliance**: Governments must comply with NIST, CJIS, HIPAA, FedRAMP, GDPR, and local data protection laws.

- **Sovereignty**: Data residency and jurisdictional control are often required.

- **Modernization**: Many agencies still rely on aging mainframes and monolithic systems.

- **Availability**: Critical services (e.g., emergency response, health portals) must be available 24/7.

- **Cost Management**: Pressure to reduce spend and increase transparency.

- **Citizen Expectations**: Digital-native citizens expect services to be mobile-friendly, responsive, and reliable.

Case 1: National Health Portal Modernization

Objective

A national health agency (referred to as "HealthGov") aimed to consolidate its fragmented digital infrastructure into a unified, citizen-facing platform providing access to:

- Personal health records

- Vaccination and immunization tracking

- Appointment scheduling

- Digital prescriptions

- COVID-19 response updates

Solution Architecture

- **Azure App Service**: Hosted the main web and mobile APIs.

- **Azure API Management**: Unified access to health records, vaccination APIs, and lab result data.

- **Azure SQL Database** and **Cosmos DB**: Stored patient data and health records with encryption at rest and role-based access.

- **Azure Functions**: Handled background tasks such as email confirmations, QR code generation, and report generation.

- **Azure Front Door**: Managed global request routing and SSL termination.

- **Azure Monitor**: Monitored latency and alerting for service degradation.

Compliance and Security

- All data hosted in regional sovereign cloud with customer-managed keys.

- End-to-end encryption enforced via TLS 1.2+.

- Integration with Azure Active Directory B2C for secure citizen login with MFA.

Outcomes

- Platform served 12 million citizens with sub-second latency during COVID-19 vaccination surges.

- Reduced legacy IT support cost by 65%.

- Enabled rapid deployment of new health initiatives using infrastructure as code.

Case 2: Judicial Case Management System

Objective

The Ministry of Justice sought to digitize case records and court management to reduce paperwork, improve access to justice, and enable virtual hearings.

Architecture

- **Azure Kubernetes Service (AKS)**: Deployed containerized microservices for case tracking, scheduling, and notifications.

- **Azure Cognitive Services**: Enabled transcription of hearing recordings and OCR of scanned evidence.

- **Azure DevOps**: Managed CI/CD for rapid deployment of features.

- **Azure Virtual Desktop (AVD)**: Provided secure remote access to court employees and legal personnel.

- **Blob Storage with Immutable Storage**: Used for tamper-proof archiving of court records.

```
resource storage 'Microsoft.Storage/storageAccounts@2022-09-01' = {

  name: 'justicestorage'

  location: 'uksouth'

  kind: 'StorageV2'

  sku: { name: 'Standard_LRS' }
```

```
properties: {

  allowBlobPublicAccess: false

  immutableStorageWithVersioning: {

    enabled: true

    immutabilityPolicy: {

      periodSinceCreationInDays: 365

      state: 'Locked'

    }

  }

 }

}
```

Results

- Reduced   average   case   handling   time   by   40%.

- Enabled   remote   hearings   during   the   pandemic.

- Improved transparency and auditability through centralized digital records.

Case 3: Smart City Initiative

Objective

A metropolitan city council deployed a "smart city" platform to enhance services such as traffic monitoring, waste management, and environmental sensing.

Solution Stack

- **IoT Hub**: Collected data from over 80,000 edge sensors (traffic, bins, air quality).

- **Azure Stream Analytics**: Real-time analytics and alerts (e.g., overflowing trash bins).

- **Azure Maps**: Visualized assets and sensor data on interactive dashboards.

- **Power BI**: Delivered KPIs to city officials for decision-making.

- **Azure Event Grid** and **Service Bus**: Orchestrated alerts and tasks between subsystems (e.g., route adjustment for waste trucks).

AI Integration

- **Azure Machine Learning** predicted peak traffic patterns and optimized signal timing.

- **Cognitive Services** analyzed images for parking violations and pothole detection.

Citizen Interaction

- Mobile app hosted on Azure App Service allowed citizens to:

  - Report issues (geo-tagged)

  - View live transit data

  - Get personalized recycling tips based on residence

Impact

- 30% improvement in waste collection efficiency

- 22% reduction in traffic congestion in downtown zones

- Increased public satisfaction ratings with digital civic services

---

Case 4: Education and Learning Management

Objective

A regional education department digitized its school system with the goal of:

- Supporting hybrid learning environments

- Managing student records and exam results centrally

- Enabling secure teacher-student collaboration

Architecture

- **Azure Active Directory B2B**: Onboarded educators securely across multiple institutions.

- **Microsoft Teams** integrated with Azure AD and SharePoint for virtual classrooms.

- **Azure App Service** hosted the Learning Management System (LMS).

- **Azure Logic Apps** automated attendance tracking and result notifications.

- **Azure SQL Elastic Pools** optimized cost across school databases.

Compliance and Privacy

- Implemented Azure Information Protection (AIP) to classify and label sensitive documents.

- Applied Data Loss Prevention (DLP) policies for email and collaboration channels.

Results

- Served over 250,000 students and faculty during the pandemic.

- Enabled digital exams with 99.99% availability.

- Reduced server procurement time from 3 weeks to 5 minutes with Azure provisioning.

Key Lessons Learned

1. **Policy-as-Code matters**: Enforcing compliance and security baselines with Azure Policy ensures consistency across agencies.

2. **Sovereign cloud offerings are essential**: Especially for government workloads requiring local jurisdiction control.

3. **Citizen authentication should be scalable and secure**: AAD B2C is key for high-volume, identity-backed citizen services.

4. **Telemetry fuels transparency**: Real-time dashboards improved internal decision-making and public trust.

5. **Modular design accelerates reuse**: Shared service components (e.g., user management, messaging) were reused across departments.

Best Practices for Government Deployments

Area	Practice
Identity & Access	Use Azure AD and Conditional Access; enforce RBAC
Data Management	Encrypt with CMK; apply retention and immutability policies
Compliance	Use compliance blueprints (e.g., FedRAMP, CJIS, NIST)
Deployment Automation	Automate with Bicep or Terraform; enforce approvals in CI/CD
Resilience	Deploy across availability zones and regions
Observability	Log every action; audit citizen access and system behavior

---

Conclusion

Governments and public sector agencies worldwide are modernizing with Azure to deliver more resilient, transparent, and user-centric services. Whether it's building citizen portals, digitizing justice systems, creating smart cities, or scaling education platforms, Azure offers the tooling, governance, and compliance posture needed to meet these high-stakes requirements. By leveraging modern architectural patterns, automation, and built-in security features, public institutions can move faster, respond to crises more effectively, and build trust with the people they serve.

Chapter 11: Future-Proofing Your Azure Architecture

Azure's Roadmap and Emerging Services

Future-proofing cloud architecture requires more than scaling today's workloads—it demands anticipating technological shifts and aligning architecture with innovation trends. Microsoft's Azure platform is continuously evolving, with new services, capabilities, and regions launching regularly to meet the demands of enterprises, developers, and governments alike. Understanding Azure's strategic direction helps architects build resilient, extensible systems that won't need major rework as the platform matures.

This section explores Microsoft's vision for Azure, recent innovations across infrastructure and platform services, and how architects can leverage these developments to maintain agility, drive transformation, and embrace continuous modernization.

Strategic Pillars of Azure's Roadmap

Microsoft's future roadmap for Azure is built around five strategic pillars:

1. **Global Scale and Reach**

2. **AI and Machine Learning Integration**

3. **Cloud-Native and Serverless First**

4. **Security and Compliance by Default**

5. **Hybrid and Multi-Cloud Flexibility**

Each of these pillars influences how services are developed, enhanced, and retired—and how architects should prepare their designs to benefit from them.

---

1. Global Infrastructure Expansion

Azure is rapidly expanding its **global footprint**, with more than 60 regions announced and availability zones in the majority of them. The growth is aimed at:

- Supporting **data sovereignty** for more countries

- Improving latency for globally distributed applications

- Ensuring redundancy and business continuity

Architecture Implications

- Use **region-paired services** to ensure automatic failover and compliance.

- Design applications with **multi-region deployment** and **geopolitical awareness**.

- Adopt **Traffic Manager** or **Front Door** for global load balancing.

Azure roadmap updates often include announcements of new regions, such as:

```
az account list-locations --query
"[?metadata.regionType=='Physical'].{Region:name,
Status:metadata.regionStatus}"
```

Staying informed on these updates ensures your applications can benefit from reduced latency and regulatory alignment.

---

2. Next-Gen Compute and Edge

Azure is investing heavily in modern compute infrastructure, including:

- **Confidential Compute**: Trusted Execution Environments (TEEs) with enclaves for secure processing (e.g., DCsv3 VMs).

- **Arm-based VMs**: Lower cost, energy-efficient compute using Ampere Altra.

- **Azure Boost**: Offloads virtualization workloads for performance improvements.

- **Azure Stack HCI and Edge Zones**: Running Azure services at the edge.

Future-Proofing Tactics

- Select VM families with future scalability and support in mind.

- Containerize workloads for portability between cloud and edge.

- Design APIs that can be hosted in **Azure Stack**, **AKS**, or **Arc-enabled Kubernetes** with minimal rework.

Example: Use Azure Resource Graph to query VM family adoption trends:

```
Resources

| where type =~ 'microsoft.compute/virtualmachines'

| summarize count() by sku.name
```

---

3. Advancing AI, ML, and Cognitive Capabilities

Microsoft's roadmap increasingly prioritizes **AI-first services** across the Azure ecosystem, including:

- **Azure OpenAI Service**: Access to models like GPT-4, Codex, and DALL·E.

- **Azure Machine Learning (AML)**: End-to-end ML operations platform.

- **Azure Cognitive Services**: APIs for vision, language, search, and speech.

- **Fabric Integration**: Bringing together Power BI, Data Factory, Synapse, and AI tools in a single SaaS layer.

Recommendations

- Expose internal data via APIs and secure endpoints for AI workloads.

- Invest in AI-readiness by modularizing data pipelines with **Data Factory**, **Synapse**, or **Databricks**.

- Use **Responsible AI practices**, including model explainability, governance, and bias mitigation.

Example: AI model deployment via Azure ML CLI

```
az ml model deploy --name fraud-detector \

  --model-id mymodel:1 \

  --endpoint-name fraud-endpoint \
```

```
--instance-type Standard_DS3_v2 \

--instance-count 2
```

---

4. Serverless and Event-Driven by Default

Microsoft continues to push toward **event-driven, serverless, and asynchronous-first computing**. This reduces infrastructure friction and speeds up delivery:

- **Azure Functions** with Durable Entities
- **Azure Container Apps** with Dapr for eventing
- **Event Grid + Service Bus** for decoupling services
- **Managed workflows** with Logic Apps

New capabilities include:

- **Workload identity federation**
- **HTTP/3** and gRPC support
- **Built-in autoscaling** in Container Apps

Architecture Implications

- Embrace **event-driven design** and **function-level modularization**.
- Build reusable serverless APIs and wrap them with **API Management**.
- Use **output bindings** and triggers to decouple logic from external systems.

Example Durable Function fan-out pattern:

```
[FunctionName("FanOutOrchestrator")]

public static async Task<List<string>> RunOrchestrator(

    [OrchestrationTrigger] IDurableOrchestrationContext context)

{
```

```
var tasks = new List<Task<string>>();

for (int i = 0; i < 5; i++)

{

    tasks.Add(context.CallActivityAsync<string>("SubTask", i));

}

await Task.WhenAll(tasks);

return tasks.Select(t => t.Result).ToList();

}
```

5. Unified Data and Analytics Strategy

Azure's roadmap includes unifying its data ecosystem under services like **Microsoft Fabric**, enabling seamless transition between analytics, business intelligence, and AI.

Key elements:

- **Data Lakehouse architecture** using Delta Lake and Apache Spark
- **Power BI integration** with real-time and AI-powered insights
- **Lakehouse security** with unified governance (Purview)
- Support for **multimodal analytics** (structured, unstructured, graph, time series)

Actions to Take

- Transition from siloed databases to unified **data lakes** with governed access.
- Use **delta tables** in Synapse or Databricks for mutable, large-scale datasets.
- Leverage **Power BI Dataflows** for self-service analytics fed from secure data sources.

Continuous Innovation in Azure Networking and Security

Azure's roadmap includes:

- **Private Link** expansion for nearly all services.
- **Azure Firewall Premium** with TLS inspection.
- **Azure DDoS Protection Standard** enhancements.
- **Zero Trust implementation blueprints.**

Recommended practices:

- Default to private endpoints where possible.
- Use NSGs, ASGs, and route tables to enforce network segmentation.
- Enable Azure Policy to detect and block insecure configurations.

Azure policy sample to deny public IPs on NICs:

```
{
  "if": {
    "allOf": [
      {
        "field": "type",
        "equals": "Microsoft.Network/networkInterfaces"
      },
      {
        "field":
"Microsoft.Network/networkInterfaces/ipconfigurations[*].publicIpAdd
ress.id",
        "exists": "true"
      }
    ]
```

```
  },

  "then": {

    "effect": "deny"

  }

}
```

Staying Aligned with the Azure Roadmap

To keep future-proofing in practice:

1. **Subscribe to Azure Updates** at https://azure.microsoft.com/updates/

2. Follow **Azure Architecture Center** for pattern changes and guidance.

3. Attend **Microsoft Build**, **Ignite**, and **partner briefings** for roadmap insights.

4. Use **Preview Features** with caution in dev/test but plan for GA adoption.

5. Maintain **landing zones** that can evolve with platform capabilities.

Final Recommendations

Focus Area	Future-Proofing Approach
Compute	Use containers and abstract execution layers (e.g., Container Apps, AKS)
Data & AI	Build for unified lakehouse architecture and integrate AI pipelines
Identity	Implement decentralized identity with AAD B2C/B2B and federated auth

Networking	Move to private endpoints and modern NSG/ASG/route setups
Monitoring	Shift to OpenTelemetry and integrated observability stacks
Deployment	Automate with GitOps, IaC, and modular pipeline strategies

Conclusion

Staying ahead in the cloud means designing with the future in mind. By aligning with Azure's strategic roadmap and adopting emerging technologies, organizations can build flexible, durable architectures that evolve naturally with the platform. This future-proofing not only reduces technical debt but ensures teams can move fast without needing to constantly re-architect as new services emerge.

In the next section, we'll dive into how organizations are integrating artificial intelligence, machine learning, and edge computing at scale—bringing intelligence closer to the data and enabling real-time decision-making.

Integrating AI, ML, and Edge Computing at Scale

Artificial Intelligence (AI), Machine Learning (ML), and Edge Computing are no longer experimental technologies reserved for forward-thinking R&D teams—they are essential tools for enterprises operating in dynamic environments. Azure provides a robust ecosystem of services that empowers architects to build intelligent, real-time, and scalable systems that span cloud and edge. Integrating these technologies enables businesses to automate decisions, personalize customer experiences, detect anomalies faster, and derive insight from data generated anywhere in the world.

This section explores the architectural strategies, service offerings, deployment models, and best practices for integrating AI, ML, and Edge Computing into your Azure-based solutions.

Strategic Drivers for AI, ML, and Edge

Business Motivations

- **Operational Efficiency**: Automate manual processes and optimize workflows.

- **Customer Personalization**: Tailor interactions in real time based on preferences and behavior.

- **Predictive Insights**: Forecast trends, demand, failures, and risks using historical and live data.

- **Real-Time Decision-Making**: Make decisions at the point of data origin (edge).

- **Compliance & Security**: Monitor sensitive environments with intelligent pattern detection.

Technical Needs

- Proximity to data for low-latency inference
- High-throughput data ingestion and preprocessing
- Flexible model training and versioning pipelines
- Distributed deployment of trained models
- Integration with cloud-native applications

Azure AI and ML Service Stack

Category	Azure Service	Purpose
Model Training	Azure Machine Learning (AML)	Train, track, deploy models with MLOps pipelines
Pre-built AI APIs	Azure Cognitive Services	Vision, Speech, Language, and Search capabilities
Responsible AI	Responsible AI Dashboard	Explainability, fairness, bias detection
Model Deployment	AKS, ACI, Azure Container Apps	Host models at scale

Inference at Edge	Azure IoT Edge, Azure Percept	Run models near data sources
Data Preparation	Azure Data Factory, Azure Synapse, ML	ETL, data labeling, and transformation
Real-time Scoring	Azure Functions, Event Grid	Trigger scoring pipelines based on events

---

Training and Operationalizing ML Models

Azure Machine Learning (AML) provides a centralized platform to manage the end-to-end ML lifecycle: from data prep and experimentation to model training, validation, deployment, and monitoring.

Key Features

- Integrated notebooks (Jupyter)
- AutoML and drag-and-drop designer
- ML pipelines for repeatable workflows
- Model registry for versioning
- CI/CD integration for MLOps

Example: Registering a model and deploying as a real-time endpoint

```
az ml model register --name fraud-detector --path ./model.pkl

az ml online-endpoint create --name fraud-endpoint --file endpoint.yaml

az ml online-deployment create --name blue --endpoint-name fraud-endpoint --model fraud-detector:1
```

Use Azure DevOps or GitHub Actions to automate the retraining and redeployment process as part of a full MLOps pipeline.

Using Cognitive Services for Turnkey Intelligence

Azure Cognitive Services provides pre-trained models via REST APIs or SDKs for common use cases:

- **Vision**: Face detection, OCR, object recognition
- **Speech**: Speech-to-text, text-to-speech, translation
- **Language**: Sentiment analysis, summarization, language understanding
- **Search**: Bing search APIs, QnA Maker (now Azure Language Service)

Example: OCR API call with Python

```python
import requests


url = "https://<region>.api.cognitive.microsoft.com/vision/v3.2/ocr"

headers = {

    "Ocp-Apim-Subscription-Key": "<your_key>",

    "Content-Type": "application/json"

}

data = {"url": "https://example.com/image.jpg"}

response = requests.post(url, headers=headers, json=data)

print(response.json())
```

These services are ideal for accelerating delivery of intelligent features with minimal investment in data science.

Edge AI: Inference at the Source

Edge computing allows inference and processing to occur **closer to the source of data**, reducing latency, bandwidth usage, and reliance on constant cloud connectivity.

When to Use Edge AI

- Remote or bandwidth-constrained environments

- Real-time response requirements (e.g., safety, automation)

- Privacy or regulatory constraints on data transmission

- Offline or intermittent network conditions

Azure Edge Capabilities

- **Azure IoT Edge**: Deploy containerized AI models to edge devices.

- **Azure Percept**: AI-enabled camera and microphone hardware for edge ML.

- **Azure Stack Edge**: On-premise edge appliances with integrated AI acceleration.

Example: Deploy model with IoT Edge

1. Convert model to ONNX or container image

2. Push to Azure Container Registry

3. Deploy to edge device using IoT Hub device twin configuration

```
"modulesContent": {

  "$edgeAgent": {

    "properties.desired": {

      "modules": {

        "aiModule": {

          "settings": {

            "image": "myacr.azurecr.io/fraudmodel:latest"

          }

        }
```

```
            }

        }

    }

}
```

Use Dapr and Container Apps for event-driven edge patterns.

Architecting Scalable AI Solutions

To support AI/ML at enterprise scale:

- Design for **modularization**: decouple data, model, and serving layers.

- Use **event-driven triggers** to invoke models in real time.

- Abstract scoring endpoints behind APIs or gateways.

- Capture **model metadata and telemetry** for drift detection and retraining.

- Choose deployment model based on latency, concurrency, and cost.

Scenario	Recommended Architecture
Real-time scoring (<100ms)	Container App or Function with ACI/AKS backend
High-volume batch scoring	AML pipeline with Data Factory trigger
Edge inference	IoT Edge with model deployment via ACR
Human-in-the-loop review	Logic Apps + Power Automate + Power Apps

---

Governance and Responsible AI

Ethical and legal risks increase as AI systems make more impactful decisions.

Governance Practices

- Use **Azure Responsible AI dashboard** for fairness and transparency analysis.

- Monitor **input and output skew** to detect model drift.

- Use **model explainability** tools (SHAP, LIME) to audit decisions.

- Maintain an **AI inventory** with documented purpose, ownership, and datasets.

- Integrate **human oversight** in high-risk use cases (health, finance, criminal justice).

Integrating AI into Line-of-Business Applications

Modern business applications are increasingly "intelligent by default." Azure enables seamless integration of AI into operational systems:

- Embed cognitive services into **CRM, ERP**, and **custom portals**.

- Use **Power Automate** to trigger flows from AI model outputs.

- Analyze logs and documents in real time with AI + Logic Apps.

- Build **AI-powered bots** for employee support using Azure Bot Service.

Use Azure Event Grid to trigger AI inference on file uploads:

```
{

  "eventType": "Microsoft.Storage.BlobCreated",

  "subject": "/blobServices/default/containers/invoices",

  "data": {

    "url":
"https://storage.blob.core.windows.net/invoices/invoice1.pdf"

  }

}
```

This pattern supports automatic extraction, classification, and routing of new documents.

Best Practices for Scalable AI/ML on Azure

Area	Best Practice
Data	Clean, label, and version data with Data Factory or Databricks
Model Management	Use Azure ML for registry, versioning, deployment, and monitoring
Deployment Strategy	Use AKS for high-scale inference, ACI for on-demand, IoT Edge for local compute
Security	Isolate models and pipelines in private networks; use managed identities
Governance	Enable audit logging and integrate bias detection tools
Automation	CI/CD with MLOps pipelines and infrastructure as code

Conclusion

Integrating AI, ML, and Edge into cloud architecture is no longer optional for organizations aiming to compete in fast-moving digital environments. Azure's unified platform provides everything needed to operationalize intelligence—from model development and deployment to edge inferencing and governance. By combining scalable infrastructure, ethical AI practices, and modern development pipelines, architects can unlock new value and resilience across virtually every domain.

In the next section, we'll turn our attention to sustainability and green cloud architecture—helping organizations not only build better systems but do so in a way that contributes positively to the planet.

Sustainability and Green Cloud Architecture

Sustainability is emerging as a foundational requirement for enterprise cloud architecture. As organizations face increasing pressure from regulators, investors, and environmentally conscious customers, building green cloud-native systems is not only an ethical responsibility—it is a strategic advantage. Microsoft Azure has committed to being carbon negative by 2030 and is empowering customers to adopt sustainable practices by offering visibility, tooling, and architectural patterns that reduce environmental impact.

This section explores how architects can design cloud solutions that are energy-efficient, cost-effective, and environmentally responsible. We will cover Azure's sustainability initiatives, green design principles, carbon-aware workloads, and best practices for measuring and optimizing the ecological footprint of your cloud applications.

Microsoft's Sustainability Commitment

Microsoft has set ambitious sustainability goals, including:

- **Carbon negative by 2030**: Removing more carbon than emitted.

- **Water positive by 2030**: Replenishing more water than consumed.

- **Zero waste by 2030**: Reuse, recycle, or compost 100% of waste.

- **Protecting ecosystems**: Creating a Planetary Computer for environmental research.

In Azure, this translates to concrete actions such as:

- Powering data centers with **100% renewable energy**.

- Implementing **liquid cooling** and **AI-optimized server design**.

- Launching tools like the **Emissions Impact Dashboard**.

- Offering **sustainability calculators** for workload-level reporting.

Designing for Sustainability: The Four Dimensions

Green architecture in Azure can be distilled into four dimensions:

1. **Compute**   **Optimization**

2. Data   Efficiency

3. Network   Awareness

4. Operational   Monitoring   and   Governance

Let's break these down with actionable strategies.

---

1. Compute Optimization

Compute is typically the largest contributor to cloud emissions. Right-sizing and optimizing compute workloads is the fastest way to reduce carbon and energy usage.

Best Practices

- **Right-size VMs** using Azure Advisor recommendations.

- Use **spot VMs** for interruptible workloads at lower environmental and monetary cost.

- Prefer **serverless** (Functions, Logic Apps, Container Apps) to reduce idle time.

- **Consolidate workloads** on fewer, more efficient compute instances.

- Use **Auto-scaling** to provision compute resources dynamically.

- Favor **ARM-based VMs** (Ampere Altra) for power efficiency.

Example: Scale-down schedule for App Service during off-hours

```
{

  "name": "ScaleDownNight",

  "properties": {

    "targetResourceUri":
"/subscriptions/{id}/resourceGroups/{rg}/providers/Microsoft.Web/ser
verfarms/myAppServicePlan",

    "recurrence": {

      "frequency": "Week",

      "schedule": {
```

```
        "weekDays": ["Monday", "Tuesday", "Wednesday", "Thursday",
"Friday"],

        "hours": [22],

        "minutes": [0],

        "timeZone": "UTC"

    }

  },

  "action": {

    "type": "Scale",

    "parameters": {

      "Capacity": "1"

    }

  }

  }

}
```

---

2. Data Efficiency

Storing and processing large volumes of unnecessary data consumes storage, compute, and energy. Data must be curated with purpose and lifecycle in mind.

Strategies

- Apply **retention policies** to purge stale logs, telemetry, and backups.

- Use **tiered storage** (Hot, Cool, Archive) based on access frequency.

- Compress and deduplicate files before storage.

- Enable **data pruning** on databases (e.g., Cosmos DB TTL).

- Avoid over-collecting telemetry—use **sampled** **logging** where appropriate.

Example: Enable TTL on Cosmos DB container

```
az cosmosdb sql container update \
  --account-name green-db \
  --database-name logs \
  --name userTelemetry \
  --ttl -1
```

---

3. Network Awareness

Network resources consume energy for transit, routing, and replication. While less obvious than compute, network design can impact sustainability.

Recommendations

- Localize traffic using **Azure Front Door** and **regional deployments**.
- Reduce **cross-region replication** where business-criticality doesn't justify it.
- Prefer **peer-to-peer traffic** within the same region or zone.
- Compress payloads using gzip or Brotli for HTTP traffic.
- Use **GraphQL** or partial response APIs to minimize over-fetching.
- Minimize redundant telemetry streams to central monitoring systems.

---

4. Operational Monitoring and Governance

You can't improve what you don't measure. Azure offers tools for tracking and managing the sustainability of workloads.

Azure Tools

- **Microsoft Emissions Impact Dashboard** (Power BI app): Reports estimated emissions by subscription, resource group, and service.

- **Azure Sustainability Calculator**: Estimates carbon impact of services like VM, storage, networking.

- **Azure Advisor**: Recommends unused or underutilized resources.

- **Azure Policy**: Enforce green architecture rules at scale (e.g., prevent large VMs, require tags for decommission review).

Example: Azure Policy to deny DSv2 VM sizes (inefficient SKUs)

```json
{

  "if": {

    "allOf": [

      {

        "field": "type",

        "equals": "Microsoft.Compute/virtualMachines"

      },

      {

        "field": "Microsoft.Compute/virtualMachines/sku.name",

        "like": "Standard_DS2_v2"

      }

    ]

  },

  "then": {

    "effect": "deny"

  }

}
```

Cloud-Native Green Patterns

Cloud-native design offers sustainability as a built-in outcome, not just an add-on.

Pattern	Sustainability Benefit
Event-Driven Architecture	Resources spin up only on demand
Function-as-a-Service	Zero idle compute
Containerization	Smaller footprint vs full VMs
Multi-tenant SaaS	Higher density utilization across tenants
Microservices	Deploy and scale independently, reducing over-provisioning
Infrastructure as Code	Eliminates zombie resources and ensures drift correction

Sustainability Metrics for Architecture Reviews

Include sustainability in your architecture review checklists alongside performance, security, and cost.

Metric	Description
Idle Time Percentage	Percent of time compute is allocated but not used

CPU and Memory Utilization	Higher is better—indicates right-sizing
Storage Overhead Ratio	Stored vs queried data volume
Cross-Region Data Transfer	MB/GB of data egress across regions
Compute Carbon Estimation (gCO$_2$)	Available via Emissions Dashboard
Number of Zombie Resources	Unused VMs, disks, NICs, IPs

Governance and Policy Framework

To scale sustainability across an enterprise, embed green principles into your **Cloud Center of Excellence (CCoE)** and cloud governance model:

- Define **sustainable architecture standards**.

- Tag resources with environmental metadata: `"sustainability":"critical"` or `"lifecycle":"temp"` etc.

- Integrate sustainability metrics into executive reporting.

- Train solution architects and developers on green patterns.

- Conduct regular "green audits" of high-impact workloads.

AI for Sustainability

Microsoft also provides AI and data platforms to support sustainability goals outside of IT operations:

- **Planetary Computer**: Open-source geospatial analytics for environmental research.

- **AI for Earth grants**: Support for climate, agriculture, biodiversity projects.

- **Azure Maps**: Location data for urban planning, pollution tracking.

- **AI models**: Forest monitoring, water quality prediction, energy forecasting.

These tools allow organizations to **embed sustainability into their products and services**, not just their infrastructure.

Final Thoughts

Sustainability is not a constraint—it's an accelerator. Cloud-native architectures, when designed intentionally, are inherently more efficient than traditional infrastructure. Azure provides both the tools and the operational model to drive measurable environmental impact reduction.

By aligning technical architecture with sustainability goals, organizations can reduce waste, meet ESG mandates, and improve operational agility. More importantly, they can contribute to a more sustainable future—without sacrificing innovation.

In the next chapter, we'll wrap up the book with appendices including a glossary, further reading, sample projects, and code snippets to help you continue your journey as a cloud architect.

Chapter 12: Appendices

Glossary of Terms

In the rapidly evolving world of cloud computing and Azure architecture, a strong understanding of key terminology is essential for effective communication, design, and implementation. This glossary consolidates the most important terms used throughout the book, offering clear and concise definitions for quick reference. Whether you're new to cloud architecture or an experienced professional looking to clarify your knowledge, this section provides a comprehensive vocabulary aligned with real-world Azure usage.

A

Active-Active   **Deployment**
A high-availability architecture where multiple systems or regions are online and processing requests simultaneously, allowing for improved failover, redundancy, and load distribution.

AKS   **(Azure**   **Kubernetes**   **Service)**
A managed Kubernetes container orchestration service that simplifies deploying, managing, and scaling containerized applications in Azure.

App   **Service**
A fully managed platform for building, hosting, and scaling web apps, REST APIs, and mobile back ends using .NET, Java, Node.js, Python, and more.

ARM   **(Azure**   **Resource**   **Manager)**
The deployment and management service for Azure. Provides a unified way to create and manage Azure resources through templates (ARM templates), CLI, REST APIs, and the portal.

B

Bicep
A domain-specific language (DSL) for deploying Azure resources declaratively, offering a more concise and readable syntax than traditional ARM JSON templates.

Blob   **Storage**
Azure's object storage solution for the cloud optimized for storing massive amounts of unstructured data such as text or binary data.

Blueprints
A service that enables rapid, repeatable creation of governed environments by combining artifacts such as ARM templates, policies, and role assignments.

C

CI/CD (Continuous Integration/Continuous Deployment)
A set of practices that enable development teams to deliver code changes more frequently and reliably through automated pipelines.

Cosmos DB
A globally distributed, multi-model database service designed for high availability, low latency, and scalable workloads.

Container Apps
A serverless container platform for running microservices, APIs, and event-driven applications without managing complex infrastructure.

Content Delivery Network (CDN)
A distributed network of servers that delivers web content and media to users based on their geographic location, improving latency and performance.

Cognitive Services
A suite of pre-built APIs for adding AI capabilities to applications, including vision, speech, language, and search functionality.

D

Dapr (Distributed Application Runtime)
A portable, event-driven runtime that simplifies building microservices by providing common building blocks for state management, service invocation, pub/sub, and more.

Data Factory
A cloud-based data integration service that allows creation of data-driven workflows for orchestrating data movement and transformation.

Durable Functions
An extension of Azure Functions that enables writing stateful workflows in a serverless compute environment.

DevOps
A set of practices and tools that integrates development and IT operations to shorten the software development lifecycle.

E

Elastic Pool (Azure SQL)
A cost-effective solution for managing and scaling multiple databases with variable usage patterns within a shared set of resources.

Event Grid
An eventing backplane that enables event-based architecture in Azure by routing events from sources to handlers.

Event Hubs
A big data streaming platform and event ingestion service capable of receiving and processing millions of events per second.

Edge Computing
A distributed computing paradigm that brings computation and data storage closer to data sources, improving response times and bandwidth usage.

F

Failover
The process of automatically switching to a redundant or standby system in the event of a failure of the primary system.

Function App
A logical container in Azure for hosting individual Azure Functions that share configuration and scale settings.

Front Door
A scalable and secure entry point for global web applications, offering Layer 7 load balancing, SSL offload, and caching.

G

Geo-Replication
A technique for replicating data across multiple geographic locations to ensure durability, availability, and low-latency access.

GitHub Actions
A CI/CD tool that allows automation of software workflows using YAML-based pipelines integrated with GitHub repositories.

Governance
The framework of policies, roles, and processes used to control and manage Azure environments at scale.

H

High **Availability** **(HA)**
A system design approach that ensures a pre-defined level of operational performance and uptime over a given period.

Horizontal **Scaling**
Increasing system capacity by adding more instances or nodes, rather than increasing the size of a single instance (vertical scaling).

I

Infrastructure **as** **Code** **(IaC)**
The practice of managing and provisioning infrastructure through machine-readable configuration files rather than physical hardware setup or interactive configuration tools.

Identity **and** **Access** **Management** **(IAM)**
Processes and technologies used to manage digital identities and control user access to resources.

Immutable **Storage**
Storage that prevents data from being deleted or modified, often used for compliance and regulatory needs.

K

Kusto **Query** **Language** **(KQL)**
The query language used in Azure Data Explorer and Log Analytics to perform read-only queries for analyzing large datasets.

Key **Vault**
A cloud service for securely storing and accessing secrets, keys, and certificates used by cloud applications and services.

L

Load **Balancer**
A networking solution that distributes incoming network traffic across multiple backend resources to ensure availability and responsiveness.

Logic **Apps**
A cloud-based platform for creating and running automated workflows that integrate apps, data, services, and systems.

M

Managed Identity
An automatically managed identity in Azure Active Directory that provides applications with access to other Azure resources securely.

Monitoring
Collecting, analyzing, and acting on telemetry data from cloud resources to ensure availability, performance, and security.

N

Network Security Group (NSG)
A set of security rules that controls inbound and outbound network traffic to Azure resources at the subnet or NIC level.

O

Operational Excellence
One of the pillars of the Azure Well-Architected Framework focused on running workloads effectively and improving support processes.

P

Private Link
A feature that enables private access to Azure services over a private endpoint in your virtual network.

Platform as a Service (PaaS)
A cloud computing model that provides a platform allowing customers to develop, run, and manage applications without the complexity of building and maintaining infrastructure.

R

Resource Group
A logical container in Azure that holds related resources for an application or workload.

RBAC **(Role-Based** **Access** **Control)**
A method of regulating access to computer or network resources based on the roles of individual users.

S

Serverless
A cloud computing model where the cloud provider dynamically manages the allocation and provisioning of servers.

Service **Bus**
A fully managed enterprise message broker with support for queues and publish-subscribe messaging patterns.

Storage **Account**
A namespace in Azure for accessing storage services such as blobs, files, queues, and tables.

T

Terraform
An open-source IaC tool for provisioning and managing cloud infrastructure using a declarative configuration language.

Traffic **Manager**
A DNS-based global traffic distribution service that directs client requests based on performance, priority, or geographic location.

U

Uptime **SLA**
Service-Level Agreement that defines the guaranteed availability percentage for a service over a specified time period.

V

Virtual **Machine** **Scale** **Sets** **(VMSS)**
An Azure compute resource used to deploy and manage a set of auto-scaling VMs.

Virtual **Network** **(VNet)**
The fundamental building block for private networking in Azure, enabling communication between Azure resources.

W

Well-Architected **Framework** **(WAF)**
 A set of principles and best practices from Microsoft for building high-quality, scalable, and resilient cloud applications.

Workbooks
 A customizable canvas in Azure Monitor for visualizing metrics, logs, and queries for dashboards and reports.

This glossary is a living resource—keep it updated as Azure continues to evolve. For additional term definitions and official documentation, visit Microsoft's Azure Glossary. In the following sections of the appendix, you'll find curated learning resources, sample projects, code snippets, and a concise API reference guide to enhance your understanding and practical implementation of the concepts covered in this book.

Resources for Further Learning

Mastering scalable cloud architecture on Microsoft Azure is a continuous journey that involves hands-on experience, ongoing education, and engagement with a growing ecosystem of professionals and tools. Whether you're preparing for certification, leading enterprise transformation, or simply looking to sharpen your skills, there is a wealth of resources available to help deepen your understanding and stay up-to-date with evolving best practices.

This section provides an extensive collection of curated learning resources—ranging from official documentation and training paths to community forums, books, events, certifications, and architecture-specific references. These resources span foundational to advanced topics and are organized to support multiple learning styles and goals.

Microsoft Learn

Microsoft Learn is the go-to platform for structured, interactive training on Azure and other Microsoft technologies. It offers:

- **Learning Paths** tailored to roles (e.g., Azure Architect, DevOps Engineer).

- **Hands-on** **Labs** using sandbox environments.

- **Knowledge Checks** and progress tracking.

Recommended paths for Azure architects:

- Designing Microsoft Azure Infrastructure Solutions (AZ-305)
- Architecting Cloud-Native Apps
- Introduction to Well-Architected Framework

You can build a personalized profile, earn badges, and access role-specific curricula to map your learning journey.

Certifications

Professional certifications validate your expertise and are often required by employers for cloud roles. The most relevant for Azure architects include:

Certification	Role Focus	Level
AZ-305: Designing Microsoft Azure Infrastructure Solutions	Architect	Expert
AZ-104: Azure Administrator Associate	Admin/Operations	Associate
AZ-400: Designing and Implementing DevOps Solutions	DevOps	Expert
AI-102: Designing and Implementing an Azure AI Solution	AI/ML	Associate
DP-203: Data Engineering on Microsoft Azure	Data	Associate

Study materials are available via Microsoft Learn, Pluralsight, Udemy, Whizlabs, and A Cloud Guru.

Documentation and Architecture Center

The Azure Architecture Center is a rich repository of:

- **Reference Architectures** with diagrams and implementation guides.

- **Design Principles** and pattern catalogs.

- **Industry-specific use cases** (e.g., finance, government, healthcare).

- **Well-Architected Framework reviews** and checklists.

Explore categorized solutions by domain:

- Compute

- Networking

- Identity

- Monitoring

- Resiliency

- Data and AI

- Migration

Each architecture includes a downloadable Visio or Bicep/ARM template for quick deployment.

Books and eBooks

Reading in-depth books can provide additional context and case studies beyond online documentation.

Top Recommendations:

- *Azure Architecture Explained* by Julian Sharp

- *Exam Ref AZ-305 Microsoft Azure Architect Design* by Ashish Agrawal and Pablo Cibraro

- *Cloud Architecture Patterns by Bill Wilder*
- *The Azure Cloud Native Architecture Mapbook by Stephane Eyskens*
- *Infrastructure as Code by Kief Morris*

Microsoft Press also offers free PDF-format eBooks for learners, such as:

- *Microsoft Azure Essentials series*
- *Cloud Design Patterns*

Check the Microsoft Press Store and Packt Publishing for the latest editions.

Video Courses and Webinars

Visual and auditory learners can benefit from structured video courses, YouTube tutorials, and Microsoft-hosted webinars.

Popular Platforms:

- **Pluralsight** (extensive Azure library, role-based learning paths)
- **Udemy** (certification-specific and project-based courses)
- **LinkedIn Learning** (soft skills + technical deep dives)
- **Cloud Academy**
- **Microsoft Reactor** (free events and coding sessions)

Microsoft's own **Azure Fridays** series on YouTube is hosted by Scott Hanselman and provides practical demos and guest interviews.

GitHub Repositories and Open Source

Real-world examples and starter projects can be found in Microsoft's official GitHub repos:

- Azure Samples: Ready-to-deploy templates and apps
- Azure Quickstart Templates: 1,000+ ARM/Bicep/IaC projects

- **Awesome Azure**: Curated list of Azure resources

- **Azure Terraform**: IaC modules and blueprints

- **Azure SDKs**: .NET, JavaScript, Python, Go SDKs

Use GitHub Codespaces or Dev Containers to clone and run examples directly in the browser.

Blogs and Newsletters

Staying current requires following thought leaders and community contributors.

Top Azure Blogs:

- Azure Blog (official)

- Microsoft Tech Community

- The New Stack

- Thomas Maurer – Cloud Advocate at Microsoft

- Troy Hunt – Security expert with Azure focus

Recommended Newsletters:

- **Azure Weekly**

- **The Morning Brew**

- **Cloud Native Weekly**

- **Serverless Notes**

- **AI & Data Weekly (by Microsoft)**

Subscribe to receive curated insights, new service releases, security bulletins, and architecture tips.

Community and Forums

Connecting with other professionals is a powerful way to accelerate learning.

- **Stack Overflow**: Get help with Azure-specific programming and deployment questions.

- **Reddit**: r/AZURE and r/devops are active communities for architecture and tooling discussions.

- **Tech Community**: Microsoft's own support forums with official staff participation.

- **LinkedIn Groups**: Join groups for Azure Architects, DevOps Engineers, and Cloud Developers.

- **Discord/Slack**: Join Azure-focused or cloud-native open communities.

Hands-On Labs and Challenges

Test and improve your skills through sandboxed environments.

- **Microsoft Learn Sandbox**: Execute scripts and labs without incurring costs.

- **Cloud Skills Challenge** (seasonal): Compete and earn badges or exam vouchers.

- **Katacoda** (now on O'Reilly): Interactive infrastructure and Kubernetes labs.

- **Hackathons**: Participate in virtual global or regional challenges (e.g., Hack the Box, Global Azure Bootcamp).

AI and Sustainability Learning Resources

As emerging priorities, AI and sustainability have dedicated learning tracks:

AI & ML:

- Azure AI Fundamentals (AI-900)

- AI School

- Responsible AI Learning Path

Sustainability:

- Microsoft Sustainability Learning Center

- Cloud   Sustainability   Calculator

Events and Conferences

Stay ahead with Azure insights from live and on-demand events:

- **Microsoft**   **Ignite**   (annual)

- **Microsoft**   **Build**   (developer-focused)

- **Global**   **Azure**   **Bootcamp**

- **KubeCon**   **+**   **CloudNativeCon**

- **Azure**   **OpenAI**   **Dev**   **Day**

Visit the Microsoft Events Hub for regional and global event calendars.

Summary of Resource Types

Category	Examples
Training Platforms	Microsoft Learn, Pluralsight, Udemy, LinkedIn Learning
Documentation	Azure Docs, Architecture Center, GitHub
Certification Prep	AZ-305, AZ-104, DP-203, AI-102
Sample Projects	Azure Quickstart Templates, GitHub Repos
Blogs & Newsletters	Azure Blog, Azure Weekly, The New Stack

| Community | Tech Community, Reddit, Stack Overflow, LinkedIn |

| Hands-On Labs | Learn Sandbox, Katacoda, Cloud Skills Challenge |

Final Thoughts

Learning Azure is a lifelong investment—there will always be new services, patterns, and tools to explore. Make time to experiment, build prototypes, contribute to open source, and attend community events. A curious mindset, combined with structured resources and real-world projects, will take you from foundational knowledge to architectural mastery.

In the next section, we'll explore hands-on sample projects and code snippets that tie together the principles and best practices outlined in this book.

Sample Projects and Code Snippets

The theoretical foundations of scalable cloud architecture are crucial, but the true test of understanding comes from practical implementation. This section presents a curated collection of hands-on sample projects and code snippets that reflect real-world use cases across various architectural domains in Azure. These examples are structured to reinforce concepts introduced throughout the book and offer templates that can be adapted for your own solutions.

Projects cover infrastructure as code (IaC), compute deployment, scalable storage, monitoring, security enforcement, serverless functions, CI/CD automation, and more. Each sample includes the purpose, structure, and relevant Azure services, along with code you can reuse in your own architecture.

Project 1: Scalable Web App with Azure App Service and Front Door

Goal: Deploy a globally accessible web application using Azure App Service, Front Door, and Application Insights for observability.

Architecture:

- Azure   App   Service   (Standard   Plan)

- Azure   Front   Door

- Azure   DNS
- Azure   Application   Insights
- Azure   Resource   Group   and   /   Key   Vault

Bicep Template Snippet:

```
resource appPlan 'Microsoft.Web/serverfarms@2022-03-01' = {

  name: 'webapp-plan'

  location: resourceGroup().location

  sku: {

    name: 'S1'

    tier: 'Standard'

    capacity: 2

  }

}


resource webApp 'Microsoft.Web/sites@2022-03-01' = {

  name: 'global-webapp'

  location: resourceGroup().location

  properties: {

    serverFarmId: appPlan.id

    siteConfig: {

      appSettings: [

        {

            name: 'APPINSIGHTS_INSTRUMENTATIONKEY'

            value: applicationInsights.properties.InstrumentationKey
```

```
      }

    ]

  }

 }

}
```

Project 2: AKS Microservices with Azure Monitor and Log Analytics

Goal: Deploy a Kubernetes cluster running multiple microservices with centralized monitoring.

Architecture:

• Azure	Kubernetes	Service	(AKS)
• Azure	Container	Registry	(ACR)
• Azure	Log	Analytics	Workspace
• Azure	Monitor	for	containers

CLI Snippet for Cluster Deployment:

```
az aks create \
  --resource-group microservice-rg \
  --name micro-cluster \
  --node-count 3 \
  --enable-addons monitoring \
  --enable-managed-identity \
  --enable-cluster-autoscaler \
  --min-count 2 \
  --max-count 10 \
```

```
--generate-ssh-keys
```

Helm Values Snippet (Microservice):

```
replicaCount: 3

resources:

  requests:

    cpu: 100m

    memory: 128Mi

  limits:

    cpu: 250m

    memory: 256Mi

livenessProbe:

  httpGet:

    path: /health

    port: 8080
```

Project 3: Event-Driven Processing with Azure Functions and Event Grid

Goal: Process uploaded files from Azure Blob Storage using an Event Grid trigger and serverless logic.

Architecture:

- Azure   Storage   Account
- Event   Grid   Subscription
- Azure   Functions   (Consumption   Plan)
- Azure   Key   Vault   for   connection   secrets

Function Code (JavaScript):

```javascript
module.exports = async function (context, eventGridEvent) {

  const blobUrl = eventGridEvent.data.url;

  context.log(`Blob created at: ${blobUrl}`);

  // Trigger image processing, data extraction, etc.

};
```

Event Grid Subscription (CLI):

```
az eventgrid event-subscription create \

  --name onBlobUpload \

  --source-resource-id
/subscriptions/{subId}/resourceGroups/rg/providers/Microsoft.Storage
/storageAccounts/myStorage \

  --endpoint
https://myfunction.azurewebsites.net/runtime/webhooks/eventgrid?code
={functionKey} \

  --event-delivery-schema eventGridSchema
```

Project 4: Infrastructure as Code with Terraform for Scalable SQL Deployment

Goal: Provision Azure SQL Database in a scalable elastic pool using Terraform.

Modules Used:

- azurerm_resource_group

- azurerm_sql_server

- azurerm_sql_database

- azurerm_sql_elasticpool

Terraform Code Snippet:

```
resource "azurerm_sql_elasticpool" "ep" {

  name                = "elastic-pool"

  resource_group_name = azurerm_resource_group.rg.name

  location            = azurerm_resource_group.rg.location

  server_name         = azurerm_sql_server.sql.name

  sku {

    name     = "StandardPool"

    tier     = "Standard"

    capacity = 50

  }

}
```

Benefits:

- Easy   to   scale
- Centralized   cost   management
- Auto-pause/resume   features   with   serverless   tier

Project 5: Secure API Gateway with Azure API Management and RBAC

Goal: Expose and secure microservice APIs behind Azure API Management (APIM) with OAuth 2.0 and usage policies.

Architecture:

- Azure   API   Management   (Developer/Consumption   Tier)

- Azure App Service (or Container App backend)
- Azure Active Directory (for token issuance)

API Policy Snippet:

```
<policies>
  <inbound>
    <validate-jwt  header-name="Authorization"  failed-validation-
httpcode="401">
      <openid-config
url="https://login.microsoftonline.com/{tenant}/v2.0/.well-
known/openid-configuration" />
      <audiences>
        <audience>api://my-api-id</audience>
      </audiences>
    </validate-jwt>
  </inbound>
</policies>
```

Project 6: Serverless ETL Pipeline with Data Factory and Azure ML

Goal: Automate ingestion, transformation, and scoring of data using Data Factory and Azure ML endpoints.

Workflow:

1. Data Factory pulls data from Blob Storage
2. Cleans and transforms using Mapping Data Flows
3. Invokes Azure ML endpoint for predictions

4. Stores results in Azure SQL Database

Data Factory Pipeline Snippet (JSON):

```
{

  "activities": [

    {

      "name": "ScoreModel",

      "type": "AzureMLExecutePipeline",

      "inputs": [...],

      "outputs": [...],

      "linkedServiceName": {

        "referenceName": "AzureMLService",

        "type": "LinkedServiceReference"

      }

    }

  ]

}
```

Project 7: Scalable Logging with Azure Monitor and Diagnostics Settings

Goal: Centralize logs from various Azure services for auditing, troubleshooting, and performance tuning.

Architecture:

- Azure Log Analytics Workspace
- Azure Monitor Diagnostic Settings

- Azure Automation / Logic Apps (for alert responses)

Azure CLI Snippet:

```
az monitor diagnostic-settings create \

  --name log-pipeline \

  --resource                    /subscriptions/{subId}/resourceGroups/my-
rg/providers/Microsoft.Web/sites/myapp \

  --workspace myLogAnalyticsWorkspaceId \

  --logs '[{"category":"AppServiceHTTPLogs","enabled":true}]'
```

Sample KQL Query for Log Analytics:

```
AppRequests

| where resultCode startswith "5"

| summarize count() by bin(timestamp, 10m)
```

Project 8: Cost Optimization Dashboard with Azure Cost Management API

Goal: Build a dashboard that visualizes resource group-level costs, trends, and forecasts.

Key Services:

- Azure Cost Management + Billing
- Power BI (optional)
- Azure REST API or SDK

REST API Example (Python):

```
import requests
```

```python
url = "https://management.azure.com/subscriptions/{subscriptionId}/providers/Microsoft.CostManagement/query?api-version=2022-10-01"

headers = {
    "Authorization": f"Bearer {access_token}",
    "Content-Type": "application/json"
}

payload = {
    "type": "Usage",
    "timeframe": "MonthToDate",
    "dataset": {
        "granularity": "Daily",
        "aggregation": {
            "totalCost": {
                "name": "PreTaxCost",
                "function": "Sum"
            }
        }
    }
}

response = requests.post(url, headers=headers, json=payload)
print(response.json())
```

Final Notes and Repository Links

To get the most value out of these projects:

- Clone the repo and deploy using your sandbox or dev environment.

- Fork and customize for your industry-specific needs.

- Use infrastructure pipelines (e.g., GitHub Actions or Azure DevOps) to automate builds.

- Implement observability from day one using Azure Monitor and App Insights.

By working through these examples, you'll gain a concrete understanding of how theoretical principles map directly to real-world implementations. The next section offers a concise API reference guide for the most frequently used Azure CLI and REST commands referenced throughout this book.

API Reference Guide

A robust cloud architecture is often built on a foundation of automation, integration, and tooling. Azure's APIs—spanning the CLI, REST, ARM templates, Bicep, PowerShell, SDKs, and service-specific endpoints—enable architects and engineers to declaratively manage infrastructure, connect services, and build scalable systems that are secure, reliable, and repeatable.

This API reference guide consolidates the most essential commands and endpoints used throughout this book, grouped by domain. Whether you're building automation pipelines, integrating third-party systems, or managing resources at scale, this guide will serve as a quick-access toolkit.

Resource Management

Create a Resource Group

```
az group create --name myResourceGroup --location eastus
```

List All Resource Groups

```
az group list --output table
```

Delete a Resource Group

```
az group delete --name myResourceGroup --yes --no-wait
```

Check Azure Subscription Details

```
az account show

az account list-locations
```

Compute: VMs, Scale Sets, and AKS

Create a Virtual Machine

```
az vm create \

  --resource-group myResourceGroup \

  --name myVM \

  --image UbuntuLTS \

  --admin-username azureuser \

  --generate-ssh-keys
```

Create a Virtual Machine Scale Set

```
az vmss create \

  --resource-group myResourceGroup \

  --name myScaleSet \

  --image UbuntuLTS \

  --upgrade-policy-mode automatic \

  --admin-username azureuser \

  --generate-ssh-keys
```

Create an AKS Cluster

```
az aks create \
  --resource-group myResourceGroup \
  --name myAKSCluster \
  --node-count 3 \
  --enable-addons monitoring \
  --generate-ssh-keys
```

Scale an AKS Cluster

```
az aks scale \
  --resource-group myResourceGroup \
  --name myAKSCluster \
  --node-count 5
```

Storage and Databases

Create a Storage Account

```
az storage account create \
  --name mystorageaccount \
  --resource-group myResourceGroup \
  --location eastus \
  --sku Standard_LRS
```

Create a Cosmos DB Account

```
az cosmosdb create \

  --name mycosmosdb \

  --resource-group myResourceGroup \

  --locations          regionName=eastus          failoverPriority=0
isZoneRedundant=false \

  --default-consistency-level Session
```

Create a SQL Database

```
az sql db create \

  --resource-group myResourceGroup \

  --server mySqlServer \

  --name myDatabase \

  --service-objective S0
```

Enable Geo-Replication for SQL

```
az sql db replica create \

  --name myDatabase \

  --resource-group myResourceGroup \

  --server myPrimarySqlServer \

  --partner-server mySecondarySqlServer \

  --partner-resource-group mySecondaryResourceGroup
```

Networking

Create a Virtual Network

```
az network vnet create \

  --name myVNet \

  --resource-group myResourceGroup \

  --subnet-name mySubnet
```

Create a Load Balancer

```
az network lb create \

  --resource-group myResourceGroup \

  --name myLoadBalancer \

  --sku Standard \

  --frontend-ip-name myFrontEnd \

  --backend-pool-name myBackEndPool
```

Create a Public IP

```
az network public-ip create \

  --name myPublicIP \

  --resource-group myResourceGroup
```

Create an Application Gateway

```
az network application-gateway create \

  --name myAppGateway \

  --location eastus \

  --resource-group myResourceGroup \

  --capacity 2 \

  --sku Standard_v2 \
```

```
  --vnet-name myVNet \

  --subnet mySubnet
```

Identity and Access

Create a Service Principal

```
az ad sp create-for-rbac --name "myApp" --role contributor --scopes
/subscriptions/{subscription-id}
```

Assign Role to User

```
az role assignment create \

  --assignee user@domain.com \

  --role Reader \

  --scope                              /subscriptions/{subscription-
id}/resourceGroups/myResourceGroup
```

Create an Azure AD Application

```
az ad app create --display-name myApp --homepage https://myapp.com -
-identifier-uris https://myapp.com
```

Serverless and Event-Driven

Create a Function App

```
az functionapp create \

  --resource-group myResourceGroup \

  --consumption-plan-location eastus \
```

```
  --runtime node \

  --functions-version 4 \

  --name myFunctionApp \

  --storage-account mystorageaccount
```

Create an Event Grid Subscription

```
az eventgrid event-subscription create \

  --name myEventSub \

  --source-resource-id
/subscriptions/{subId}/resourceGroups/myRG/providers/Microsoft.Stora
ge/storageAccounts/myStorage \

  --endpoint
https://myfunction.azurewebsites.net/runtime/webhooks/eventgrid?code
={key}
```

Trigger a Logic App via HTTP

```
POST      /workflows/{logicAppName}/triggers/manual/paths/invoke?api-
version=2016-06-01 HTTP/1.1

Host: {region}.logic.azure.com

Authorization: Bearer {access_token}

Content-Type: application/json


{

  "data": {

    "userId": "1234",

    "event": "signup"

  }
```

```
}
```

Monitoring and Observability

Create Log Analytics Workspace

```
az monitor log-analytics workspace create \

  --resource-group myResourceGroup \

  --workspace-name myWorkspace
```

Enable Diagnostics Settings

```
az monitor diagnostic-settings create \

  --resource
/subscriptions/{id}/resourceGroups/myRG/providers/Microsoft.Web/site
s/myApp \

  --workspace myWorkspaceId \

  --name diagnostics \

  --logs '[{"category":"AppServiceHTTPLogs","enabled":true}]'
```

Sample KQL Queries

App Performance Logs:

```
requests

| where duration > 500

| project timestamp, name, duration, resultCode
```

Azure Function Failures:

```
exceptions
```

```
| where cloud_RoleName == "myFunction"

| where type == "System.Exception"
```

Security and Compliance

Enable Defender for Cloud

```
az security auto-provisioning-setting update --name default --auto-
provision "On"
```

Set Policy to Enforce Tagging

```
az policy definition create \

  --name require-tag \

  --rules require-tag-rules.json \

  --params require-tag-params.json \

  --mode All \

  --display-name "Require Environment Tag"
```

Cost Management and Optimization

Get Current Subscription Usage

```
az consumption usage list --start-date 2023-01-01 --end-date 2023-01-
31
```

Forecast Future Cost

```
az consumption forecast list --timeframe MonthToDate
```

List Budgets

```
az consumption budget list --resource-group myResourceGroup
```

DevOps and Automation

Create a GitHub Action Workflow (YAML)

```yaml
name: Deploy Bicep Template


on:
  push:
    branches: [main]


jobs:
  deploy:
    runs-on: ubuntu-latest
    steps:
      - uses: actions/checkout@v2
      - name: Login to Azure
        uses: azure/login@v1
        with:
          creds: ${{ secrets.AZURE_CREDENTIALS }}
      - name: Deploy Bicep
        run: |
          az deployment group create \
            --resource-group myResourceGroup \
```

```
--template-file main.bicep
```

Final Notes

This guide presents just a subset of the APIs most relevant to scalable architecture in Azure. For more comprehensive documentation:

- Azure   CLI   Reference

- Azure   REST   API   Reference

- ARM/Bicep   Resource   Schema

- Azure   PowerShell

Whenever possible, prefer **idempotent, declarative infrastructure management** via IaC over imperative scripting to ensure consistency and compliance.

In the final section, we will explore frequently asked questions that arise during architecture reviews, exams, and enterprise cloud adoption initiatives.

Frequently Asked Questions

Navigating the complexities of scalable cloud architecture on Microsoft Azure often leads to recurring questions—whether from new architects entering the field, teams undergoing cloud transformation, or organizations aiming for enterprise-grade performance, compliance, and operational maturity. This FAQ section compiles detailed answers to the most common and critical questions that arise throughout cloud solution design, deployment, governance, and optimization.

The questions are categorized across key domains: architecture design, scalability, identity, cost, security, automation, DevOps, observability, and compliance.

Architecture & Design

Q: How do I choose between PaaS and IaaS when designing applications in Azure?
A: The decision depends on control, maintenance, and complexity. PaaS (like App Service, Azure SQL) offers faster deployment and automatic updates, ideal for stateless, modular workloads. IaaS (like VMs) offers more control, suited for legacy migrations, OS-level configuration, or workloads requiring custom runtime environments. Consider hybrid use with

containerized apps on AKS or Azure Container Apps when modularity and portability are needed.

Q: When should I use Azure Kubernetes Service instead of Azure App Service?
A: Use AKS when you require:

- Microservices with independent lifecycles

- Advanced traffic routing and service meshes

- Helm charts, persistent volumes, and affinity rules

- CI/CD with multiple environments

Use App Service for simpler web apps, APIs, or backend services without complex orchestration or infrastructure dependencies.

Scalability

Q: What's the difference between horizontal and vertical scaling in Azure?
A: Horizontal scaling (scale out/in) adds or removes instances, ideal for stateless apps or services behind a load balancer. Vertical scaling (scale up/down) adjusts resources (CPU, RAM) of a single instance. Azure supports both, but horizontal scaling is preferred for resilience and elasticity. Always design with statelessness to maximize horizontal scalability.

Q: How can I implement auto-scaling in my solution?
A: Azure provides auto-scaling for:

- App Services (based on CPU, memory, schedule)

- VM Scale Sets (based on metrics or schedules)

- AKS via Kubernetes autoscaler

- Azure Functions (event-driven scaling) Configure scale rules in the Azure Portal, via ARM/Bicep, or programmatically using `az monitor autoscale`.

Identity & Access

Q: What's the difference between Azure AD and Azure AD B2C/B2B?
A:

- **Azure AD**: Enterprise identity and access management (IAM) for internal users.

- **Azure AD B2B**: Federation for external business partners (guest users).

- **Azure AD B2C**: Custom-branded identity service for consumers (social and local accounts).

Q: How do I enforce least privilege across my Azure subscriptions?
A:

- Use **RBAC** to assign granular permissions.

- Apply **management groups** to enforce policy across subscriptions.

- Regularly audit roles using **Azure AD Privileged Identity Management (PIM)**.

- Avoid using `Owner` unless necessary. Instead, use `Contributor`, `Reader`, and custom roles.

Cost Optimization

Q: How can I reduce Azure costs without compromising scalability?
A:

- Use **Auto-scaling** to avoid over-provisioning.

- Opt for **serverless** or **consumption plans** for event-driven apps.

- Move infrequently accessed data to **Cool/Archive tiers**.

- Use **Azure Reservations** and **Savings Plans** for long-running workloads.

- Monitor spend with **budgets**, **alerts**, and **Cost Analysis**.

Q: How do I track cost by team or project?
A:

- Apply **tags** (`Project`, `Department`, `Owner`) consistently.

- Use **Azure Cost Management** to filter costs by tags.

- Enforce tagging policy using **Azure Policy** to prevent untagged resource creation.

Security & Compliance

Q: How do I secure public endpoints like App Services and Function Apps?
A:

- Use **Private Endpoints** to isolate services within a VNet.

- Enforce HTTPS-only connections.

- Enable **WAF** via Azure Front Door or Application Gateway.

- Configure **IP restrictions**, authentication via Azure AD, and OAuth 2.0 policies in API Management.

Q: What's the best way to secure secrets in my architecture?
A:

- Store secrets in **Azure Key Vault**.

- Use **managed identity** to access Key Vault from your app.

- Rotate secrets using **Key Vault events** and automation.

Automation & IaC

Q: What's the difference between ARM, Bicep, Terraform, and Pulumi?
A:

- **ARM**: Azure's native JSON-based declarative template language.

- **Bicep**: A more readable DSL for ARM, designed by Microsoft.

- **Terraform**: HashiCorp's cloud-agnostic tool, popular for multi-cloud.

- **Pulumi**: Infrastructure as Code using general-purpose programming languages.

Choose Bicep or Terraform for most modern Azure-native deployments. Bicep integrates directly into Azure CLI and Portal with native support.

Q: How do I prevent configuration drift in my environments?
A:

- Use **IaC** with version control (Git).

- Automate deployments via **CI/CD** **pipelines.**

- Use **Azure** **Blueprints** or **Terraform** **state** **locking.**

- Periodically run compliance scans with **Azure Policy**, **Defender for Cloud**, or **Terraform** **plan.**

DevOps & CI/CD

Q: How can I implement CI/CD for an Azure Function or Web App?
A:

- Use **GitHub** **Actions** or **Azure** **DevOps** **Pipelines.**

- Define YAML workflows to deploy via `az functionapp deploy` or `az webapp deployment`.

- Integrate testing, linting, and artifact packaging into the pipeline.

- Use **staging** **slots** to test safely before swapping to production.

Q: **Should** **I** **use** **separate** **subscriptions** **for** **environments?**
A:

- For large organizations, yes. Use separate subscriptions for `Dev`, `Test`, and `Prod`.

- Use **management** **groups** and **policies** for governance.

- Smaller teams may isolate via **resource groups** and naming conventions within one subscription.

Observability & Operations

Q: How do I monitor performance and availability of my architecture?
A:

- Use **Azure Monitor** and **Application Insights** for metrics and tracing.

- Enable **Log** **Analytics** and query with **KQL**.

- Use **Azure** **Alerts** to notify via email, webhook, or Logic App.

- Visualize insights in **Workbooks** or export to **Power** **BI**.

Q: **How** **can** **I** **implement** **distributed** **tracing** **across** **microservices?**
A:

- Use **OpenTelemetry** with Azure Monitor Exporter.

- Instrument services with Application Insights SDK.

- Ensure correlation IDs (`traceparent`) are passed across services and queues.

Disaster Recovery & Business Continuity

Q: What's the difference between High Availability (HA) and Disaster Recovery (DR)?
A:

- **HA** ensures application uptime under normal failures (e.g., using availability zones, scale sets).

- **DR** ensures recovery after catastrophic failures (e.g., geo-replication, backup restores).

Implement both:

- Use **Availability Zones**, **Load Balancer**, **SQL zone redundancy** for HA.

- Use **Geo-paired storage**, **Azure Site Recovery**, **Azure Backup** for DR.

Governance & Policy

Q: **How** **can** **I** **enforce** **governance** **across** **multiple** **teams?**
A:

- Use **Management** **Groups** to organize subscriptions.

- Apply **Azure Policy** for tagging, allowed VM SKUs, region restrictions.

- Use **Azure Blueprints** for standardized deployments with pre-approved artifacts.

- Integrate **Defender for Cloud** for security posture monitoring.

Best Practices

Q: What are the top five mistakes to avoid in Azure architecture?
A:

1. Hardcoding secrets and connection strings (use Key Vault).

2. Ignoring tagging and naming conventions (for tracking and automation).

3. Over-provisioning resources "just in case" (instead, use auto-scale).

4. Designing everything as monoliths (leverage microservices or functions).

5. Not planning for observability (use logs, metrics, and alerts from day one).

Q: How should I prepare for architecture review meetings?
A:

- Prepare architecture diagrams (logical, physical, data flow).

- Include documentation on scalability, security, cost, and DR.

- Address the Five Pillars: Cost, Reliability, Performance, Security, and Operations.

- Highlight trade-offs and decisions made during design.

Final Thought

FAQs are living knowledge—update them regularly based on architecture reviews, support tickets, retrospectives, and project post-mortems. Encourage team-wide contributions to shared knowledge bases, Confluence pages, wikis, or runbooks.

This concludes the book's appendix and reference materials. You are now equipped with both the strategic understanding and the practical tooling needed to architect scalable, secure, and sustainable solutions on Microsoft Azure. Continue exploring, building, and iterating—cloud excellence is a continuous journey.

www.ingramcontent.com/pod-product-compliance
Lightning Source LLC
LaVergne TN
LVHW051434050326
832903LV00030BD/3086